alibaba

The Inside Story Behind Jack Ma and the Creation of the World's Biggest Online Marketplace

Liu Shiying and Martha Avery

COLLINS BUSINESS
An Imprint of HarperCollins Publishers

HarperCollins books may be purchased for educational, business, or sales promotional use. For information, please write: Special Markets Department, HarperCollins Publishers, 10 East 53rd Street, New York, NY 10022.

All photos provided courtesy of Alibaba (China) Co., Ltd.

FIRST COLLINS EDITION PUBLISHED 2009

Designed by William Ruoto

Library of Congress Cataloging-in-Publication Data

Liu, Shiying.
Alibaba : the inside story behind Jack Ma and the creation of the world's biggest online marketplace / Liu Shiying and Martha Avery.
—1st Collins ed.
p. cm.
Includes index.
ISBN 978-0-06-167219-4
1. Internet auctions—China. 2. Alibaba (Firm) 3. Ma, Jack, 1964–
I. Avery, Martha. II. Title. III. Title: Inside story behind Jack Ma and the creation of the world's biggest online marketplace.
HF5478.L58 2009
381'.142092—dc22
[B]
2008035721

09 10 11 12 13   OV/RRD   10 9 8 7 6 5 4 3 2 1

Contents

Martial Arts Moves

Alibaba was founded by a man named Jack Ma in 1999, in Hangzhou, China. This is the story of how he leveraged his initial capital of $60,000 into a company valuation of billions of U.S. dollars in less than ten years. More than that, it is the story of an unlikely hero—short, scrawny, unaristocratic, and poorly educated—who saw an opportunity, a dream, and scrambled to make it real.

On November 6, 2007, Alibaba.com approached the public for funding: it issued shares on the Hong Kong stock market in an IPO, or initial public offering. The listing was to receive $1.5 billion at the offering price of HKD (Hong Kong dollars)

13.50 ($1.74). The share amount represented 17 percent of the total value of one part of the company, since only 17 percent of Alibaba.com shares were allocated to the public listing. The total valuation of Alibaba.com stood at $10 billion at the offer price, but on the day shares were issued, they rose to HKD 39.50, putting the valuation of the company at nearly $26 billion.

Jack Ma failed the college entrance examination in China twice; he barely passed on the third try. He believes that if he has been able to succeed, most people can do the same. But not everybody has set out to restructure the way business is done around the world by creating a new model for use of the Internet. By systematically putting together the elements of a new model, what he calls an "ecosystem," Jack Ma started a global movement from a small corner of China. He enabled millions of small companies to use the Internet as a primary business tool, to a degree allowing Internet functions inside China to evolve beyond what they are in the West. Through use of this tool, he has effectively leveraged China's ability to trade; over the past several years, this has changed the weighting of China on the world's stage.

Despite Jack Ma's "anyone can do it" claim, the fact remains that not just anyone did. The following chapters address the question of what he did that was different. They describe the story of a scrappy child in southern China who embarrassed his parents by fighting and by failing, who had no educational background in IT industries or business, and whose management style leans heavily on stories of historical outlaw heroes from China's past. Martial arts devotees will enjoy much of what Jack Ma feels is the secret to success.

Almost everything about Jack Ma is counterintuitive—he looks at the world from a unique perspective. His greatest delight is using small to conquer big, quick to conquer slow, and intuitive insight to conquer conventional wisdom. The abstractions by which he formulates strategic plans are based on the moves of martial arts more than mathematical equations, and the mental discipline behind those moves informs his every thought. In Jack Ma, we are looking at the incarnation of a traditional martial arts master.

Alibaba.com is only one of the network of companies under the Alibaba umbrella. Others include an online payment service called Alipay, the largest online payment platform in China, and an online consumer marketplace called Taobao, which has all but chased eBay out of China. They include a software development company called Alisoft, which creates business software that "lives" on the Net. All of these lie within the embrace of the Ali family and are ultimately controlled by Ali management and employees. Key investors in the network include Softbank in Japan and Yahoo! in the United States. The founders of those companies have been keys to Jack Ma's vision of creating a global company—but one that is owned by and managed by Chinese nationals.

In reading Jack Ma's story and the story of Alibaba, it is useful to place the company in the context of global Internet business. Up until the end of 1995, China officially forbade any news about the Internet in Chinese media. By 1997, however, this policy was overturned, and the steep curve of Internet use in China had begun. Today, there are more than 230 million Internet users in the country, according to the government-backed China Internet Network Information Center (CNNIC). China has more Internet users than any other country, including the United States, which it surpassed in early 2008. More than one-half of China's users, more than 163 million, are connected via broadband, due to the remarkable fiber backbone that the Chinese government has funded throughout the country. China's telecom growth has also been driven by the expansion of mobile telephony, which contributes to wireless Internet access as well.

While China has one of the most sophisticated Internet filtering technologies in the world to censor information, the decentralization of information technologies and their creative use for nonpolitical purposes ensure the Chinese people rapid entry into a digital age. Jack Ma's recognition of the potential for the technology allowed him to develop a model that was self-sustaining and economically viable. It focuses on ways information technology can make small companies more competitive and profitable. Since four-fifths of business in China is done by some thirty-two million small companies, the leveraging effects are substantial. Jack Ma's model is discussed in this book, but perhaps his biggest lesson for the world is his approach to innovation and implementing innovative ideas.

Put Up Your Fists!

There are two sides to every fight, and both invariably get hurt in a battle. Jack Ma does not understand this conventional wisdom, for he loves a good fight. The tougher the fight, the more he enjoys it, and the harder the work, the happier he becomes. The logic may seem strange to some, but Ma has followed this approach since he was a boy.

Jack Ma was born on September 10, 1964, into a family that lived on the shores of West Lake in Hangzhou. Ma legend has it that his family was common and ordinary, but ordinary families do not live on the shores of West Lake. Ma's mother and father spent their lives as professional performers of *ping tan*, a traditional style of storytelling and ballad singing performed in Suzhou, in southern China.

As a result of this background, Ma grew up speaking the Suzhou dialect with his parents, and he has strong attachment to the city and the traditions of that historic place. Suzhou has two kinds of people, as the saying goes: one kind loves to talk, and the other loves to listen. One does not have to look far into Ma's background to find the roots of his astonishing ability to extemporize onstage and his ability to inspire high performance through his speeches. From childhood, Ma watched and absorbed the training of professional performers, especially his parents. His own performance style may be attributed to that early exposure: Ma uses simple and direct language to explain precisely what he means. He wastes no words—and he gets to the point.

Nonetheless, Ma was not the kind of child who liked to talk much or have anything to do with achievement. Like many boys his age, he was regarded as a rebel: stubborn, naughty, incorrigible, the kind of boy who had to be disciplined repeatedly, but even that discipline did not change him. Much of this striking out against others may have had to do with his status as a social outcast. The Cultural Revolution in China began shortly after Ma was born, and he grew up in an environment of extreme social tension. The family was on the wrong side of political correctness: Ma's grandfather had been affiliated with the Kuomintang (KMT), the side that lost in China's Communist-vs.-KMT civil war. Ma was therefore the child of a family that, legally and morally, was regarded as beneath the concern of society.

The family was classified as belonging to the "five blacks," meaning the five categories of people who had earned the hatred of the masses. These groups included landlords, rich peasants, counterrevolutionaries, evildoers, and rightists, all of whom could be loosely summarized as people on the wrong side of the political spectrum. Methods of persecution against the five blacks included beating and torture.

Perhaps to mute a kind of rage against the world in which he found himself, Ma immersed himself in the lore and romanticism of martial arts novels. These are called *wu xia* novels in Chinese. *Wu* refers to things martial, and *xia* (pronounced *shia*) are people adept in martial arts but also steeped in a chivalrous approach to justice, people who belong to a brotherhood of like-minded outlaws. The link between *wu xia* novels and Ma's heritage is simple: the great outlaws of Chinese lore (as in the great sixteenth-century Chinese novel *Outlaws of the Marsh*, also known as *Water Margin*) operated around the lakes and rivers of southern China, specifically in the Jiangsu and Zhejiang regions. Suzhou is in Jiangsu; Hangzhou is in neighboring Zhejiang. The novel incorporated folktales and legends from as early as the twelfth century. By maintaining a profound emotional link with the past, Ma was able in his childhood to ride through a desperate period of social unrest in China.

Social unrest during the Cultural Revolution was a product of many factors including, for a large segment of society, personal and prolonged acquaintance with hunger. The problems of the period known as the Three Years of Natural Disaster in China were originally attributed to natural causes, but are now understood to be due partly to natural disasters and some 60 percent to mismanagement. These hard years began after the Great Leap Forward of 1958, when national policies disrupted the normal raising and distribution of food. In the ensuing years of famine, some thirty million people are said to have died as a direct or indirect result of not having enough to eat. Children born during or shortly after this harsh time were unavoidably stunted in their natural growth. Ma's diminutive size may or may not have resulted from malnourishment, but his feisty nature is evidence that, however challenged, he was determined to survive.

Perhaps because he was so small, Ma always wanted to become a kind of martial arts master in life. Profoundly influenced by *wu xia* novels, he fought with anybody who gave him any reason to put up his fists, but he fought mainly to stick up for and defend his friends, an acceptable code of honor to him.

The unfortunate thing about Ma's pugnacious attitude toward life was that he was, and remains, skinny and short. He fought often, and he often lost. "I was scrawny when I was young, but I was a terrific fighter," Ma says of himself. "I was never afraid of opponents who were bigger than I." He was badly wounded a number of times, and once had to be taken to the hospital to get stitched up and put back together again. Since there was no anesthesia at that time, he gritted his teeth and came through with an even stronger will.

Nobody among teachers, neighbors, and family held out any hope that a boy who so loved to fight would amount to much in the future. His friends were the only ones who disagreed: they considered him a righteous hero. From an early age, Ma had been able to create a cohesive bond among a select group of peers.

There is an old adage in Chinese that says one can see how big the man will become when the child is just three, and one can see what the old man will look like when he is seven. Ma's character was formed quite early, and anyone looking at him at the age of seven would have recognized one or two key traits. He hated mediocrity, falseness, and bullying. He would not tolerate injustice, and clearly, during the Cultural Revolution, injustice surrounded him pervasively. Too, he was determined to work for ideals: perhaps because of the influence of *wu xia* novels, he was fully convinced of the power of right-minded dreams.

"Men are made bigger by adversity and injustice" is one of Ma's favorite sayings. Ma was in a difficult position at home, since his parents were understandably trying to escape criticism and keep a low profile. When Jack came home bloody after another fight, his father whipped him with a bamboo rod. Ma notes today that he tried hard to hold himself back from fighting, mostly because he did not want to stir up trouble for the family and did not want his parents to be disappointed in him. At times, apparently, the bullying became too great. The gang of his rivals in Hangzhou often used psychological tricks to goad him into a fight. One incident has become famous in the lore surrounding Jack Ma: security forces came to the family home, targeting Ma's grandfather but at the same time using Maoist language to criticize the young boy. They told him he had better behave, or else. The rivals had sneaked up and were watching from outside the windows. The next day, at school, when the teacher used the same phrase from the Maoist textbook, a schoolmate shot Ma a snickering look. Ma threw his textbook at the boy, the boy in turn threw his book bag at Ma, and a battle ensued. And so we can see that Ma grew up fighting for his family name; he grew up in the midst of struggle.

Mathematics vs. English

People say that if you want to change the world, you should first change yourself. Ma seems to have done the opposite: he changed the world but preserved himself much as he was. He started out small and unremarkable, which he remains, and while he initially struggled with math, he was a whiz in English—and this is still true today.

Different from other children from the beginning, he was not particularly charming or adorable, and he got terrible marks, generally failing math. The strange thing was that he had unbelievably fluent English: in the 1970s and 1980s, when math and engineering trumped humanities, this was not the way teachers thought things should be. Ma's stubbornness and his bellicose nature naturally influenced his studies. In middle school, however, he was fortunate to have a likeable young woman as his geography teacher. Her teaching style was natural and lively, and she often told stories about herself in order to illustrate her points. Once she told a story that benefited Ma for years to come, to the point that he believes it actually changed his whole life.

The story was quite simple. One day, the teacher was walking along the shore of West Lake and some foreigners asked her to tell them about Chinese geography. Her English was good enough that she could respond intelligently. "You all have to study geography," she told the students, "but even more important is for you to study English. For when foreigners ask you something and you can't answer them, you will make all Chinese people lose face."

Ma went home to pick up some money, and on the very same day spent six *mao,* around two U.S. dollars at the time, to buy a radio. He used this to listen to the English broadcast every day. Ma was twelve years old when he started applying himself to learning English. Nowadays most Chinese children would feel that starting English at the age of twelve was too late. Back then, when the policy of opening and reform had not yet begun and nobody knew what political movement might be coming next, studying English at the age of twelve was a precocious decision.

Ma's parents had no English at all. They could not write the alphabet and so they were no help in his self-study. His efforts ran up against many obstacles, but he carried on mainly because he so thoroughly enjoyed the language. He soon started haunting the shores of West Lake, trying to latch onto foreigners with whom he could practice speaking English. From the start, he was thick-skinned when it came to making mistakes. Soon, people who talked to him would push the glasses back on their noses to take another look: they assumed that he was an overseas Chinese recently returned to the mainland.

In the course of this self-study, Ma made quite a few foreign friends. Two of them were critical in his understanding of Western thinking and will be discussed later. Others taught him much about the outside world, even though he had never put one foot outside the gates of China. After starting college, Ma would still regularly seek out foreigners in hotels with whom to carry on conversations. His many years of diligence laid the foundations for a high degree of competence and cultural understanding.

Ma remembers his early student days fondly. If you ask him what he is most proud of, he will tell you stories relating to his accomplishments in English. He'll tell you about using his pedicab to serve as an English-speaking guide for foreigners at the age of thirteen. He'll tell you about his mistakes and how they didn't kill him—his mantra seems to be that you may have problems, but if they don't kill you, you can always get up and start again. However, other than being admired by people for his English prowess, Ma will not tell you about anything else he experienced in those years because it was not an easy time.

Ma Goes to College

Compared to luminaries of the Internet in China, men whose names include Jiang Nanchun, CEO of Focus Media, and Chen Tianqiao, CEO of Shanda, Jack Ma had an arduous path to college. Jiang Nanchun was sent to East China Normal College just because of one essay for which he won a prize. Chen Tianqiao graduated from Fudan University on the strength of being an outstanding young soldier in Shanghai. Both of these men are now regarded as among the richest in China, their wealth measuring more than $1 billion. In contrast, Ma never went to a first-rate middle school or grade school, let alone college. All were third- or fourth-tier institutions. Even more interesting, he took the college entrance examination three times and failed the first two.

After failing the examination the first time, Ma began a delivery service with his pedicab. He also applied to work in a hotel but was turned down because he was so short. But after many setbacks and tremendous determination he finally succeeded in getting into college. Since he has become famous, Ma has not been reticent in talking about these failures. On the contrary, he likes to use his own failures to encourage others. He jokes that his own failures in college exams might give hope to those whose marks are bad and who need a boost to their self-confidence. Ma believes firmly that you have to take hold of your own life and make it into something, not wait passively for events to happen. He also believes that this can make a success out of most anyone. "I am really rather stupid," he says. "My brain is so small that I can only think of one thing at a time. If you ask me three things in a row, I can't absorb them."

In passing tests and getting into both high school and then college, Ma's biggest hurdle was mathematics. The Chinese policy at the time adhered to what is described as a "wooden bucket theory," and college admissions were ruled by this theory. The capacity of the bucket was determined not by the length of the longest staves around its sides but by its shortest. One's total score, or "capacity," had to be defined by one's lowest marks, not one's best. Ma's longest "short staves" were so short that in effect his whole bucket could contain very little. His shortest staves were, of course, in math. He simply couldn't figure out how to do math.

The first time Ma took the college exam, he got a mark that signified total defeat. Head hanging down, he went to work as a hired laborer. As mentioned earlier, he responded to a hotel help-wanted ad; he and his cousin, who was tall and handsome, went together. The cousin was hired, but Ma went home rejected. After that, he worked transporting things, including magazines for three publishers with whom his father had connections. He would ride his pedicab over and pack magazines, twenty-five to a bundle, then ride the ten kilometers to the train station that shipped the magazines to other places.

One day, Ma was hired to help copy documents at an institution called the Zhejiang Dance Troupe Association. Here, he got hold of a book called *Life*, by the author Lu Yao. Fate may well have determined the serendipitous appearance of this book. It so influenced Ma that it changed his thinking in short order and helped guide the future course of his life. Just as Lu Yao's later book, *A Common World*, influenced a generation of young people in the 1970s, *Life* influenced all who lived through the 1960s. Its hero, Gao Jialin, was a so-called intellectual living in a farming village. Although talented, Gao was not able to achieve his ideals in life. He tried hard, but something always happened to push him backward just when he was reaching a new stage. As a result, he never had the opportunity to develop his talents.

Ma saw himself in this sad story. More importantly, he saw that the path of life is long, but there are critical moments when things change, and the outcome of those moments can be determined in a very short time. Nobody's life is a straight line, everyone faces forks in the road, and most of life is filled with tribulations. Precisely because of this, people should face forward with optimism and not be surprised when they encounter problems. They should recognize that they can ride over these problems, laugh at life with courage, and use their own enthusiasm to create their lives. This profoundly optimistic approach to life may have been enhanced by a reading of Lu Yao, but *Life* may also have been just the catalyst to allow Ma to exercise his own native instincts.

Now Ma decided that he would try again to get into college. He began preparing a second time for the exam. China's college entrance exams were given once a year. The practice of national exams had been reinstated in 1978, after a hiatus of more than a decade. As an indication of how hard it was to get into college, the following statistics from the Ministry of Education are illustrative: 6.1 million people registered for the exam in 1978, 5.8 million people took it, and of these millions, a total of 402,000 people were admitted to institutions of higher education. In 1980 and 1981, when Ma was taking the exam, the huge initial bulge of aspirants had not yet worked its way through the system, so it is not surprising that many excellent candidates were rejected.

Ma took study courses in the summer of 1980, bicycling back and forth between his home and the school. At the second exam, Ma's math mark came up from 1 to 19, still far below the passing grade. Even worse, this second failure discouraged his parents. They had held on to the hope that he might go to college; now they asked him to go out and find a job.

For the next year, Ma worked days and studied at night, and spent every Sunday in the library at Zhejiang University. Here he was to meet six of the key people with whom he is happily working in the realm of e-commerce today. This time, when he prepared for the exam, Ma took a different approach to math: he memorized formulas and equations as if he were memorizing literature. The age-old practice in the Chinese scholastic tradition is to memorize and recite literature: all classics have been studied in this way, and Ma simply followed this ancient way.

Three days before the third exam, one of Ma's professors, Professor Yu, said to him in a somewhat discouraging way, "Ma Yun, your math is dreadful. If you pass this time, I will start writing my name upside down." This had the salutary effect of making Jack Ma angry, but it added to his determination to actually pass math; it was something he remembered for many years.

In contrast to such pessimism was another incident that Ma remembers, which resonated far more deeply than any negative approach. A young woman from the countryside had such spirit that she was invited to be on the TV program *Dialogue,* of comparable fame to the *Oprah* show in the United States. In the course of the show, this young woman, whose education reached only through the second year of middle school, said, "There will be light in your eyes only if there are dreams in your heart." This was more in line with Jack Ma's beliefs. He took the exam for the third time, and this time he passed. On the morning of the exam, he had chanted aloud the ten basic mathematical formulas, and during the exam he applied them, one by one. Coming out of the exam, he compared answers with his classmates and knew that he definitely had come up to the mark. This time, his math grade was 79—not high, but enough to squeak through.

To most people in China, a mark of 79 in math would seem pathetic; to Jack Ma, it was above the passing mark of 70, and that was what counted. Unfortunately, it was still not high enough for him to be allowed into the general college curriculum, known in China as *ben ke*. China divides college into regular courses of study and a more limited occupational-education college. Ma was permitted only to take the more limited curriculum. However, now that the god of good fortune had started smiling on Jack Ma, he helped him along even more. The rolls for *ben ke* at Hangzhou Normal University were not totally filled, so Ma was allowed to enter the *ben ke* program there. He was assigned to study foreign languages.

The comments of Professor Yu may have spurred Ma on to greater efforts: we do not know if that statement about writing his name upside down was made with good intentions or not. We do know that Jack Ma was already well on his way to becoming a pro at disregarding the doubts and opposition of others. He has often stated, "People who don't like me, or who are opposed to people like me, are very much against us. Those who appreciate people like me are very much for us. I don't want everyone to like me, and that could never be the case anyway. But if everyone was against me, that wouldn't necessarily be bad. What I most despise are attitudes in the middle, the 'middling.' I am against mediocrity in every way. And the degrees by which I measure may be different. Say, for example, that the degree of your endurance for having people not like you is twenty million. Someone else's may be thirty million. Mine would be two hundred million." Ma's ability to "take it" stood him in good stead, and he had finally been admitted to college. He entered college with tremendous excitement and curiosity. His path there could be called a route from life to death and back again.

College and a Dream

In 1984 Ma was twenty years old. He had finally, with his "block-head energy," been allowed to stride through the gates of college. The college he entered was not impressive or famous; in fact it could not have been more ordinary. The term *normal* in the name Hangzhou Normal College refers to an institution that prepares people to teach school, generally middle or high school. Ma was generously allowed to enter the regular full curriculum: he was told he was being allowed to "join the ranks of revolution," allowed to "reform himself."

Both the English language and the idea of teaching fit him perfectly. Spoken English was his strong suit, and he took to college as a fish takes to water. He sailed smoothly along, wind at his back, heart full of enthusiasm, and body full of martial arts vigor. With the simple opportunity to go to college, Ma began his quest for the outstanding in life. From the day he entered college, fate began to smile upon him. He found the classes easy and realized that he did not need to spend all his time studying. As a result, he began to involve himself in the student union and was soon elected its president. Later, he was elected president of the entire League of Student Unions of Hangzhou. To a student from the lower tier of colleges, this was something of a miracle.

Many of his peers looked at this transformation and at what Ma has since gone on to accomplish, and wonder how it all happened. "This is the same guy who used to eat in our dining hall," they say, "but there he is, and here we are, still sleeping away on the same old campus."

Ma himself has strong opinions about achieving success. He says, "I personally know that others are better at calculating than I am. I know that others can also talk better than I can. But I was quite successful in college and I have been successful in founding a company. Therefore, I tell young people, if Jack Ma can be successful, I believe that 80 percent of people can also be successful."

Part of Ma's success comes from his ability to rouse people's enthusiasm, and he attributes that ability to his years of teaching. "The ability to stand up and speak in front of people was developed, trained into me, in the process of my teaching. Now, when I get up onstage I don't prepare. The minute I open my mouth, I can't hold back what I have to say." Ma's ability to talk is as famed in Internet circles; he is known worldwide as stylish, charming, and frank. After founding Alibaba, this man who was Hangzhou born and bred and had never left its environs was able to go abroad and, in the most carefree, easy manner, win customers and supporters among Americans and Europeans.

When Ma graduated, he was the only one among five hundred graduates of the *ben ke* program to be placed as a teacher in a higher institution. The others were placed in middle or high schools. He was appointed to teach at the Hangzhou Electronics Technology College. There he spent the next five years, conscientiously teaching English to young people. He would not have lasted that long had he not made a promise to one of his mentors, an older man who came to visit him early in his career. This leader from a local institute knew that Ma, restless and ambitious, might be inclined to head out on his own, as many of his peers were doing. Jack Ma felt that commitments were binding. He took to heart the request by his elder and promised he would stay for five years, and he did.

In the course of those five years, Ma became famous locally as a dynamic and irresistible professor. Students would cut classes just to come see him "perform." The results of his teaching style were quite astonishing: students who had little foundation in English soon found that they were opening their mouths and speaking a foreign language. Ma is proud of his techniques. "I have analyzed Li Yang's 'Crazy English,'" he says of Li's unorthodox method of teaching English, "and if I had joined in that business I could have topped him. My tricks truly are able to make a person speak a foreign language." During this time, however, many of Ma's peers were setting up businesses or going abroad. And so, in addition to teaching at the Hangzhou Electronics Technology College, Ma began teaching night classes to friends involved in foreign trade. This put him in touch with the wider world of business; it also allowed him to form a core group of comrades, several of whom remain Alibaba's key personnel today.

Darkest Before Dawn

J ack Ma is the kind of man a mother has to worry about. He calls himself lazy. He quit a good job. Just when he seemed to settle into one stable career, he switched to another. When he makes a decision, he often overturns it. According to friends and observers, his life has been an endless series of revisions. That he is now one of China's wealthiest and most influential men may be a tribute to this restless roaming.

The revisions began when he was a young man. In 1988, he graduated from Hangzhou Normal College and settled into teaching English at Hangzhou Electronics Technology College.

He was drawing a respectable salary and enjoyed the work, then surprised everyone by abandoning this line of work and starting a translation company.

In 1994 Jack Ma turned thirty, the age at which a person in China is regarded as having come of age to the degree that he should be set up on his own. This Confucian saying is known to all and generally observed. The dean of the college in which he was teaching had promised Ma that some day he would be appointed head of its External Affairs Department. Rejecting this very promising future, Ma resigned soon after and set up a company called Haibo. Its name was chosen for its aural similarity to the English word *hope*. In English, the company is now known as the Hangzhou Hope Translation Agency.

The Haibo Translation Agency can be seen as the first evidence that Jack Ma, as many were to learn, "never gives in." This mantra was calligraphed next to his photograph on the Haibo Web site. The site was primitive, but it started the trajectory that led to Ma's fame today. The Web site text read: "The Hangzhou Haibo Translation Agency was established in January 1994, founded by Jack Ma. The State Administration for Industry and Commerce granted the company permission to register as an organization specializing in translation. Haibo is the first such organization to be established in Hangzhou." It went on to note that principal early customers included the Hangzhou municipal government and the judiciary of Zhejiang Province.

Haibo still exists and is run by a woman named Zhang Hong. She recalls her entry into the company years ago. "Back then, nobody else saw the opportunity in this business. Ma Yun saw it: he has phenomenal foresight. We didn't make much money at first, but Ma persevered, and saw through to where he wanted to be. I respect him tremendously, for he has a great ability to motivate people, and he can invest things that seem hopeless with exciting possibility. He can make those around him get excited about life."

Ma himself says that he started the business because he wanted to be a better teacher. "Everything I taught was drawn from knowledge in books. I wanted to spend some time in actual practice, learning to distinguish between what was true, or real, and what wasn't. I decided to put ten years into setting up a company, and then I intended to come back to the school to teach, with a better understanding of what I was doing."

An Unremarkable Student Becomes an Outstanding Businessman

Ma realized that there was a need for translation when friends kept coming to him, asking him to translate things. With little free time of his own, he began to use others—what he calls "hired guns"—to do the work. The hired guns were mostly retired professors, who could make a modest living in this line of work. At first, Ma felt he was doing a kind of public service, particularly since the company lost money—it was paying out in rent twice what it was bringing in. Employees began to waver in their decision to work for the company, and for a time morale was dismal.

To shore up income, Ma personally went out on the street to peddle things, anything by which he could turn a profit: flowers, books, clothes, flashlights. The trade helped supplement the income of the translation house during its early, rocky period. The determination of the core group of people who co-founded the company with Ma also helped revive the morale of employees. According to Ma, the company was breaking even by the end of 1994 and had begun to turn a profit in 1995. Ma was generally considered a fool at the time. He himself acknowledges that he learned from his many mistakes. He did accomplish two things: he kept alive a translation house that provided a useful service, and he successfully organized Hangzhou's first English Corner, a place to congregate for practicing the language. Today, Haibo is Hangzhou's largest translation house. Its services have been indispensable in the foreign-trade component of the company Alibaba.

"I knew that there was a need, and so I realized that it should actually not be so hard to succeed," says Ma today. That vague sense of optimism was about the extent of his strategic planning in starting the company. In the early stages of Haibo, he continued teaching at the Electronics College in addition to teaching night classes. Those classes were to play a crucial role in his later founding of Alibaba, for his students were Hangzhou traders and businesspeople of all kinds. The founding and management of Haibo also contributed lessons to his later business: "The process made me realize that those who succeed need two qualities. One is a forward-looking personality that is fairly confident, not to say courageous. The other is a keen sense of the market."

Ma Goes to America

Ma's first contact with the Internet was during his initial month-long trip to the United States in 1995. This trip had qualities of gangster movies and slapstick at the same time. Many details remain murky. In Ma's own description, "It was really like a classic American-style Hollywood film. I was taken hostage by a kind of Mafia, so that [when I escaped] I just left my suitcase behind—it's still back there somewhere."

This is how it all came about. The Hangzhou municipal government was in the process of building a highway between Hangzhou, in Zhejiang Province, and Fuyang, in Anhui Province. An American investor had been talking to transportation department authorities, negotiating a deal, but talks had stalled and no money had appeared. Both sides felt that there must be problems in communication, and Hangzhou authorities thought of the excellent English-language capabilities of Jack Ma. At the time, he was known as one of the best English-speakers around, and was marginally more familiar with things foreign than others in Hangzhou. Ma was chosen to serve as both interpreter and mediator in the business talks. As he became more familiar with the situation and delved more deeply into the considerations, he found that it was, as he states, "a particularly complex story."

The American investor was to receive compensation in the form of toll rights, which meant he could collect fees from the finished road. This method of paying back the cost of building a road was not uncommon; it was similar to the way the Hong Kong businessman Li Ka-shing had financed the building of a road from Wutong to Shenzhen, near Hong Kong. The method was acceptable in terms of both theory and practice. The devil was, as usual, in the details.

Problems began during the building of the highway. More than one thousand people were soon working on the road, but as time went on they found they had been working for a year without any pay. The Chinese began to realize that even American bosses practiced unethical behavior, cheating construction crews of their pay. The Hangzhou municipal government therefore authorized Jack Ma to serve as intermediary along with a representative from the American side, who described himself as having come "to serve as a communications channel to resolve the problem." According to this American, the problem lay in the fact that the Hong Kong board of directors was balking—it would be necessary for Jack Ma to go to Hong Kong to talk to them. Hong Kong was still a British colony in the mid-1990s, and was the site of many headquarters and offices of companies doing business with China.

Ma went to Hong Kong and discovered that all was not as

the American had said. Back in Hangzhou, the American now said that it was the *American* company's board of directors who were creating the problem. With no other recourse, the Hangzhou authorities agreed to send Jack Ma to the United States to talk to those directly in charge. He applied for a visa and to his surprise actually got one (at that time visas were not easy to get), and off he went. The next month was to be "inhuman in its tragedy," as he described it. "Every strange and bizarre thing that could happen did happen."

Ma soon discovered that the American had been deceiving Hangzhou all along, that he was a "dyed-in-the-wool cheat"—that, indeed, he was known in the States as an international swindler. He and Jack Ma then traveled to America together, and the swindler took Ma to see "the investors." In the short time that Ma spent with them, he heard somebody mention the Internet. He already had a vague impression of the Internet from an Australian teacher back in Hangzhou, so his mind was prepared when the word crossed the screen again.

The American boss now took Ma to Las Vegas to gamble. Since Ma was carrying out the mission entrusted to him by the Hangzhou municipal government, he did not pay much attention to "other things that happened at the time." One thing about the gambling proved significant, however: Ma gambled $25 at the slot machines and won $600. Using these winnings, he was eventually able to start on his path to the Internet. In the meantime, he found he had been placed under *ruanjin*, or "soft detention," in his room. It had become apparent to the American that Ma knew he was a swindler, and that defeat was looming: Jack Ma fully intended to return to Hangzhou to let the cat out of the bag.

The American began to work on Ma, trying to persuade him to come in with him as partner. He even tempted him with an annual salary of $100,000. Ma refused. The American then continued to keep Ma locked in his room, not bothering to have any further communication with him. Like any ordinary person, Ma was not going to agree to being locked up and hungry for too long. According to his rendition of the story, he called the American and negotiated. "If you want me to go back and work on your behalf, then your terms have to be improved. I want you to invest in another business of mine." He then told the American he had plans to develop an Internet site. The American had little understanding of this high-tech concept, but he agreed to have Jack Ma "check it out" once he got back to China.

Once released, Ma lit out for home. He left the hotel without even bothering to pick up his suitcase, taking only the six hundred dollars he had made in Las Vegas. Ma said of the swindler he left behind, "The man was rotten to the core. He was later found to be on the wanted list and was in the end arrested by Interpol." No further information on this man or his relationship with Hangzhou has surfaced.

First Personal Contact with the Internet

Every man has his own game plan. Yahoo!'s Jerry Yang has his; Softbank's Masayoshi Son has his. Before 1995, Jack Ma's game plan was to be a professor of the English language. After 1995, it was to go out in the world and meet up with the Internet. On escaping from the clutches of the American swindler, Ma took a plane from Los Angeles to Seattle instead of going straight back to Hangzhou. Once in Seattle, he went in search of a small Internet service provider (ISP) named VBN, whose young workers he had heard about. He found their offices: two small rooms, in which five people sat before computers, madly putting together Internet pages.

Ma was uncomfortable even touching a computer back in 1995. The young people at VBN sat him down before one and coached him in how to access the Internet. In those days, the information technology associated with the Internet was primitive: the browser the young people used was something called Mosaic, while the largest search engine in the States at the time was Web-Crawler. Mosaic had been released to the general public in 1993, after being developed by the National Center for Supercomputing Applications. It was funded by a bill put before Congress by Al Gore, Jr. WebCrawler was the creation of a man named Brian Pinkerton at the University of Washington, who released it on April 20, 1994. It was the first search engine to index entire pages, and it became so popular that often it could not be used during the day, only late at night. AOL eventually bought the company out. Meanwhile, also in April 1994, David Filo and Jerry Yang had just created their Yahoo! Directory and in the coming months began offering it to others for a fee. For little Jack Ma, from way out in Hangzhou, China, it was indeed exciting to be accessing the cutting edge of all this technology.

As Ma remembers it, the VBN people asked him what he wanted to look up on the Internet. They said, "Type it here." He typed in "beer." The results came back with German beer, American beer, Japanese beer . . . but no Chinese beer. Then he typed in "Chinese" and the results came back "no data." He looked for other things Chinese—still "no data." This interested him. Before, he had only heard about the Internet, since it was not available in China. Yet here he was, actually using it, touching it, experiencing it. He began to develop his idea of starting a company in China that was specifically related to the Internet and to things Chinese.

Ma's first Web pages were made in the United States, not in China. The first page was the extremely primitive page for Haibo. On it were prices for translations and a telephone number. This was the start. Without it, there might have been no Jack Ma talking happily these days about global e-commerce and IPOs. Creating a Web site in China at the time was hardly possible because

China did not have a regular system for licensing ISPs in 1995. The Ministry of Information Industries, or MII, was established only in 1998 to serve as an impartial regulatory agency, under which was placed the former monopoly power of the Ministry of Posts and Telecommunications. The MII was authorized to review, approve, and grant licenses for ISPs later that year. In late 1999, its director at the time, Wu Jichuan, noted that regulation of ISPs would be under the MII while regulation of Internet content would be under other government agencies, those specifically concerned with information flow and propaganda. From the beginning of the Internet in China, any IT entrepreneur had to navigate multiple layers of authority.

Ma remembers distinctly that the Haibo page was finished at 9:30 A.M. one day when he was in the United States, and by evening he had received five e-mails. He was tremendously excited. Three were from people in America, two of whom were overseas Chinese. This was the first Web page they had ever seen about products in China. The other two were from Japan, and they asked about pricing. Ma was essentially illiterate when it came to the Internet, but his business sense told him that there was a play to be made here. He had a sense that the Internet would be changing the world, and he wanted to be in on it.

He grasped the essentials of his mission early on: pull together information on Chinese enterprises, put it on a Web site, and broadcast their products to the world. He decided to work together with his American friends at VBN on the technical side of the business. He mentally sketched out a global business-to-business (B2B) e-commerce model and began work.

In China, full-function connection to the Internet started in 1994. Professor Qian Hualin at the Academy of Sciences in Beijing had spearheaded this effort and presided over the establishment of the Chinese domain name system. But that was in Beijing, at the heart of the scientific establishment and governmental support. Ma lived in Hangzhou, far from the technology centers of Beijing and Shanghai. As an outsider, he was a particularly precocious innovator in China's Internet businesses.

Now clear on what he was doing, Ma returned to America and met with potential partners. "Let's cooperate," he said. "You be responsible for technology on the American side; I'll go back to China, pull in customers, and do promotion." Ma had already chosen a name for the project: it was the Chinese equivalent of "China Yellow Pages," while the English name for his Web site was Chinapage.

The Haibo Network

The very night Ma returned to Hangzhou, he invited twenty-four friends to a meeting. All were students in the night school where he taught; all worked in the field of foreign trade. Having taught them English, Ma understood their needs and knew how helpful a Web site for promotion of their products could be. His idea, however, met with little enthusiasm. Of the twenty-four, twenty-three said it was too early to get into this business. "It won't work," they told him.

"I spoke for two hours," Ma said later, "and they didn't get it. I myself didn't know what I was talking about. One person said he would take a chance, but if it didn't work he would turn tail right away. So I thought about it for one night. The next morning, I decided to do it. Even if twenty-four had been opposed, I would have carried on."

One factor in his decision was a sense of giving it a try. Ma has always felt that one does not measure success just by the results; instead, he feels that the experience of doing something is in itself a kind of success. "You go out and charge around . . . if it doesn't work, you can always bow out. But if you just think over thousands of things at night and in the morning keep on walking the same old path, you never get anywhere. You don't grow. You might as well try." Ma has often commented on the fact that he is praised less for his acumen than for his courage.

Most people in China had no idea of the Internet in 1995. Even in the United States, Nicholas Negroponte did not publish his famous book *Being Digital* until 1995. Jerry Yang and David Filo had created Yahoo! in 1994 while at the same time studying for graduate degrees at Stanford, but by 1995 they had received $1 million in investment and were devoting all their time to the Internet. In China, there was no way to dial up and reach the Internet from Hangzhou, and it was hard from most other places. Beijing had started a connection from the Academy of Sciences, but information was strictly controlled. It was not surprising that Ma's friends opposed the idea of making an actual business out of this situation.

In April 1995, Ma put $800 of his savings (RMB [renminbi] 7,000*) into a pot for the new company. He got his sister, his brother-in-law, his parents, and other relatives to pitch in too, and he came up with $2,380 (RMB 20,000). From this small beginning, the China Yellow Pages became one of China's earliest Internet companies.

The "Trickster" and His Yellow Pages

Ma was regarded as a kind of trickster as he went around to businesses trying to get them to spend money promoting themselves on the Internet. He obviously was trying to pull the wool over

---

*Conversions between RMB=USD are noted according to the exchange rate at the time.

their eyes, people thought. He went out every day to sell his Yellow Pages, to get people to agree to be advertised on the Internet. But what was the Internet? Nobody believed him. "What sort of nonsense is this? Yellow what?"

Ma would respond, "China Yellow Pages, on the Internet. It's that high-speed information highway."

They would say, "I see. You're looking for Mr. X. Over there."

"Which room?"

"The next one down, the Comprehensive Department."

So Ma would go to the man in the Comprehensive Department, who would say to him, "I'm telling you, this is very complex. Things to do with these so-called Yellow Pages, they're not as simple as you imagine."

Complexity in China often has to do with government regulations and de facto social prohibitions. The market economy itself was highly government-influenced at the time, and anything to do with information industries belonged wholly to the government. The complexities were multilayered and would have smothered anyone less determined to slice through red tape. In February 1996, for example, the State Council promulgated Interim Regulations on Management of Computer Information Networks—International Connections. These required that all users, individuals and organizations, strictly follow the State Secrecy System. The State Secrecy Bureau followed up with a State Secrets Protection Regulation in 2000. In August 2002, the MII required ISPs to monitor more closely any use of the Internet: software was to be installed by ISPs that allowed recording of all messages. If messages were suspect, the ISP was to notify MII under penalty of law. All of these rules and regulations meant that the public was wary of anyone trying to deal with the political issues and make money off something as dangerous as the Internet. They didn't want to get involved.

There was also criticism of Jack Ma's selling style. When he talked, he seemed all hands and feet, no grace. Hangzhou people are known for their civility and their sophisticated suavity; Ma had none of that and indeed was often described as a country bumpkin. Way back in 1995, the whole business was a very hard sell.

"It was pitiful. It was like trying to cheat someone, but not really. We'd tell everyone, 'There is this thing, you see,' and then we'd try to describe it, this and that. Later I came to understand that old saying about how a rabbit eats the grass nearest his burrow first. At the beginning, therefore, I put up information for friends. They knew my credibility over the years was pretty good. Eventually they would agree to come on board with some payment. The very first to agree was the Lakeview Hotel in Hangzhou, a four-star hotel. Second was the Qianjiang Law Offices, and third was the Fourth Electrical Machinery Plant of Hangzhou."

Without direct access to the Internet, Ma used his contacts in America to do the uploading. "We came to the Lakeview Hotel and asked the staff for printed material on their business. We immediately sent that by courier to America, and the technical people there put it into the Web page. At the time, we had a basic standard price for putting up information: $2,380 [RMB 20,000] for a photograph and text up to three thousand words. After the American side finished work, they would print a hard copy of what the page looked like and they would courier it back to us in China. Before sending the material to America, we would have had it translated into English, which is where the Hope Translation House came into play. So we did all this and we took the hard-copy printout of the Web page to the Lakeview Hotel manager and told him his hotel was up on the Internet. He didn't believe us. We said to him, 'This is an American telephone number on the Web page. You can ask your friends in America to call this number and find out if it's really there or not. If it isn't, come after me. If it is, then you have to pay the fee.'"

Ma enjoys narrating in detail the tribulations of "playing a zither for a cow," as the Chinese have it, over the course of that year. He was preaching to the deaf, but one or two early believers heard the message. Slowly but surely, Ma created a business. The Lakeview Hotel story turned out well. In 1995, the U.N. Fourth World Conference on Women was being held in Beijing; attendees from other countries went on the Web before coming to China to try to find out about China's hotels. The only one they could get any information on was the Lakeview—so they all came to the Lakeview for a holiday after the convention.

In July 1995, Shanghai set up a dedicated Internet line with a dial-up number. Ma decided to get online directly from Hangzhou, in order to prove to his customers that he had not cheated them. He got everyone in a room, with a 486 computer, and he made a long-distance call to Shanghai. Then he began to download photos and information on the Lakeview Hotel from the American site. It took three and one-half hours. (These days young people sometimes complain about the Internet being too slow. Back then, the maximum connection speed was 24K— nobody who lived through that period complains very much today.) When a photo from the hotel finally began to appear on the screen, Jack Ma burst out crying. He was so happy and so excited that he simply couldn't help it.

Ma's second customer was the Qianjiang Law Office. "I had a friend there who was one of my students. We made a Web site for him, but he still didn't believe it was up there," Ma recalled. "So he put his own home telephone number on the Web page. His phone soon began ringing off the hook. Some foreigner was trying to talk to him in English. My friend was amazed, and he bought into the Yellow Pages."

By August 1995, China Telecom started an Internet service in Shanghai. Ma followed up with a Yellow Pages there too. His registration number was 7. "In those days, you'd have to use something called PPT to make a long-distance call via computer, which I didn't understand at all. You had to write down a whole long list of things." The service is easier today: China Telecom, one of China's two main providers, is by now the world's largest wireline telecommunications and broadband services provider. Its shares are listed both on the Hong Kong and the New York stock exchanges.

China Yellow Pages began to make money. Soon it was set up in twenty-seven cities throughout China. Ma would initially be regarded as a swindler by people in any city that had no direct access to the Internet, but he kept at it. "I would remind myself every day that the Internet right now is like a hundred-meter dash that is going to be influencing people's lives for the next thirty years. So I have to run like a rabbit. But at the same time I have to have the patience of a tortoise."

The China Yellow Pages gained a measure of fame after setting up Web pages for places such as the Little Goose Pagoda in Wuxi and the Guo-an Football Stadium in Beijing, sites in which the general Chinese public had great interest. By the end of 1997, operating income from the Web site reached the unimaginable figure of $830,000 (RMB 7 million). Looking back, one can see the embryonic form of Alibaba in the learning curve associated with the China Yellow Pages.

Going to Beijing

As the Internet developed in China, Jack Ma found that competition was quickly entering the business. Several major competing Internet initiatives were launched just as his own China Yellow Pages was finally reaching respectable levels of income.

One was a company called Edison, launched with an investment of $20,000 from Nicholas Negroponte at the Massachusetts Institute of Technology (MIT). Zhang Chaoyang had earned his Ph.D. from MIT and returned to China to start that company with Negroponte's help. Charles Zhang, as he is also known, was the same age as Ma but followed a very different path in life. He was born in 1964 in Xi'an, Shaanxi Province, but passed his exams with flying colors and took his B.A. from Qinghua University in Beijing. The recipient of an international scholarship in 1986, he joined a privileged group of students at MIT. There he received a Ph.D. in experimental physics. Zhang returned to China in 1995, started a company that was later renamed Sohu, and launched the sohu.com Web site in February 1998. It went public on Nasdaq in the year 2000, before the collapse of the dot-com bubble torpedoed everyone else. As CEO of Sohu, Charles Zhang has gone on to be named a Global Leader of Tomorrow by the World Economic Forum and achieve recognition as a fellow architect of the future—from such people as Jack Ma, who was to cooperate closely with Sohu in later years.

Another man, Wang Zhidong, had developed a company called Star of China. Wang was one of those precocious software developers who could develop a marketable product in a matter of weeks. He is famed for writing the first Chinese-language software for PCs. In late 1998, he merged his company with a Silicon Valley–based portal set up by three Taiwanese students from Stanford. This was the start of the portal sina.com.

Yet another developer, Chen Tianqiao, had taken the Lujiazui Group public by listing on the Shanghai Stock Exchange. His company allowed people to peruse news on the Internet. Chen later developed Shanda Interactive Entertainment and by 2005 was regarded as one of the ten richest men in China. He owed this transient reputation in part to the listing of his interactive online gaming company on the Nasdaq exchange.

Ma looked on all these developments with great interest, then decided to enter the major leagues by taking his company to Beijing. Shanghai had opened a dedicated line for the Internet in July 1995. Nevertheless, Ma had continued to rely on the American side for development work in creating Web pages and the overall site. One day, by chance, he received a CV in the mail along with corporate information that was to go on the Internet. Ma read the CV, invited the man over, and soon engaged him to create a Web site design. Within a week, the man had made a passable Web site. The man's name was Li Qi, and he was to figure prominently in the success of Alibaba. Li Qi is now chief operating officer of the company Alibaba.com. "This site was in fact ugly as could be," Jack Ma was later to say, "but we were overjoyed since we knew that now we could create our own. We soon severed relations with the partners in the United States."

The reason was expense. The American side had been wanting 60 percent of the money, and it was far more economical to do the work inside China. People were beginning to notice the promise of the Internet: the company Ying Hai Wei ("1+Net"), known as the front-runner in China's Internet world, was soon followed by a company called Wan-wang, and then by China Telecom and ChinaNet. Jack Ma's comment about these competitors was: "We couldn't kill them, and they couldn't kill us. We all just had to carry on."

Ma's early appreciation for publicity garnered results. In 1995, he hired one agency to do all the publicity for the launching of the Web page created for Zhejiang Province, spending $238,000 (RMB 2 million) of his client's money. This was China's first government-involved project, and it drew attention from as far away as Washington, D.C., and the U.S. Congress, which sent congratulatory telegrams. Yang Jianxin, head of the Taiwan Office in the Zhejiang Provincial Government, was of considerable help in this project, not by extending funds but by giving recognition to Jack Ma.

Ma began to face harder times when he got to Beijing later in 1995. He and his general manager for sales, He Yibing, paid visits to the leading Internet figures of the day including, most importantly, Zhang Shuxin, a woman who had founded China's first ISP a full two years before China Telecom and ChinaNet. She was a pioneer in the early development of the industry.

While 1+Net served as an important stepping-stone in the development of the Internet in China, Ma's evaluation of the company was that it was focusing unrealistically on a "people's network," whereas he was trying to make an "enterprise network." Zhang Shuxin talked about theoretical things, whereas Ma was more pragmatic. Ma met with her for little more than thirty minutes. After leaving, Ma told He Yibing, "If anyone is going to be killed on the Internet Highway, she will certainly be a casualty before I will." Ma has never been known to mince his words, and he had it right. Ying Hai Wei was purchased in 1996; it had tremendous losses in 1997; Zhang Shuxin resigned in 1998; and the company itself closed in 2004. These days her area of Zhongguancun has completely changed. From being fields back then, it is all skyscrapers now. Once a synonym for China's Internet, Zhang Shuxin's company is a thing of the past, simply one of the many shards of China's history.

Navigating government policies was one of the trickiest aspects of growing an Internet company in the early days. By mid-1995, it is estimated that only forty thousand people were accessing the Net in China. This number came to the attention of the authorities, however, and by early 1996 regulations restricting use were being passed. In March 1996, the Ministry of Public Security released a circular notifying people that all users had to go through a procedure of registering with authorities within thirty days of establishing an Internet link. Those who had already been using the Internet had thirty days to do the same. They had to register through their local Public Security Bureau. This had both positive and negative connotations, but many at the time regarded the "legitimization of Internet use" as positive. Any rule allowing use of the Internet was a step forward. Many knew that the government would unavoidably put stringent controls on the Internet. At the same time, all knew that if China wanted to develop high-tech industries, its government had to figure out a way of accommodating this new technology.

Media Promotion

After meeting with Zhang Shuxin, Jack Ma returned to Hangzhou. In December, he resumed his "attack" on Beijing by attempting to mobilize a media campaign. He believed that winning support and recognition of the general public was going to be critical to success. He and his sales director took various materials up to Beijing and began asking friends and acquaintances to help spread the word.

At that time, it was not easy to get publicity for private purposes in China. All media is still officially state-owned or state-controlled. Newspapers are restricted in what they can print, and in 1995 the controls were far more stringent. Advertising was just beginning in the mid-1990s; advertising on television began only in 1993. Getting publicity meant getting out what was known as "soft news," articles in papers that publicized a company but were not strictly news. One of China's larger-circulation papers at the time was the *Beijing Youth News*. Ma found out that a friend of his knew a car-service driver for the *Beijing Youth News*, and he used this tenuous connection to pull his way into the limelight.

It should be understood that corporate drivers in China were in a privileged position at the time, and still are to a degree. Drivers have daily access to senior people; they are trusted, and in state-owned organizations they are not insignificant in influencing minor things. Ma met with the driver and, with great hopes and expectations, handed all the material on his company over to him, together with $60 (RMB 500). He told the man, "It doesn't matter what form the publicity takes. All we want is to get China Yellow Pages out in the public eye. Details are up to you." The driver was successful: not long afterward, the *China Trade News* published an article on Ma's company and the Internet. Mention of the Internet was not generally allowed in Chinese media at the time; Ma was impressed by the driver's success and amazed at the courage of the paper's editor. He decided he had to meet this person.

When the two started talking, and they kept on talking for three days and three nights. Like Jack Ma, the editor understood the significance of the Internet; although he knew next to nothing about it, he was aware it would be important. He told Ma, "I am going to help you out." He then invited a number of people in the media to come hear Ma speak.

Ma put out $3,500 (RMB 30,000) to host thirty journalists and editors at a dinner at the club associated with the Ministry of Foreign Trade and Economics (MOFTEC, also known in reorganized form as MOFERT, Ministry of Foreign Economic Relations and Trade). He had prepared two computers with information on their hard disks. The slow speed of transmission in Beijing at the time made direct access to the Internet impossible, so he had copied two Web pages onto these hard disks.

The experience proved to be an exhilarating success. Ma had never seen so many journalists in one place together at one time. He spoke for two hours and the journalists, though barely understanding, were wildly enthusiastic. They responded with a promise to publicize his company. All parted with good feelings, but the next day the leaders in the state offices governing media sent down a document forbidding any mention of the Internet in any way. This was at the end of 1995. It was rumored that members of an institute had put the kibosh on the initiative, advising the government that the prospects for the Internet were not good, and the technology was in any event too advanced for conditions in China. So much for the Internet.

Ma felt this was nonsense. Furious, not least because of the time and money he had put into his efforts, he asked some of the journalists what could be done. They said that if he could get the state's main propaganda organ, the *People's Daily*, to put a Web page up on the Internet, then they could report on that. This now became his goal.

Getting the *People's Daily* on the Internet

Ma went from exhilaration to despair to steely determination. He told He Yibing, the sales director, "One day I will march into Beijing." He Yibing told him that he personally was, on the contrary, ready to throw in the towel. He'd had enough. Then he told Ma that only by following the journalists' suggestion of getting the *People's Daily* on the Internet would Ma be able to rectify the situation and, at the same time, advertise himself. Getting the *People's Daily* to do a Web page was an illusion back then, a wild pipe dream. The chances of succeeding in the mission were near zero, but He Yibing had hit Ma's competitive nerve, and now Ma decided to make it happen. Starting at the end of 1995, he traveled repeatedly to Beijing to meet with various people. One time he took along Li Qi, the technology man from Shenzhen who had made that first Web page for him. Li Qi remembers the conviction with which Ma repeated that he was going to march into Beijing.

Finally a friend introduced Ma to an administrator in the General Office of the *People's Daily* in early 1996. They met at the paper and talked until late at night. Around 10:00 P.M. someone poked his head in the door and asked what the two of them were talking about. "The Internet," said Ma, and the man came in to join them. Only later did Ma find out this was Gu Jiawang, soon to become head of the Future Development Department of the paper. Gu had studied abroad and knew a bit about the Internet, so he and Ma hit it off right away. He soon recommended that Ma give a lecture to colleagues at the paper.

Based on this lucky chance, Ma was able to lecture twice at the *People's Daily*. He spoke of how China was a latecomer to the Internet, the last train in the station. He spoke of how the best defense was an offense, that China had better get itself prepared. By the end, he was exhausted, not so much worried he had failed as because he had whipped himself up so much in the course of the speech. On his conclusion, one of the leaders came over and shook his hand. "You spoke well," he said. "Tomorrow I am going to send a report up to Central. I'm going to recommend that the *People's Daily* put a Web page on the Internet."

The commotion that attended this new development in China's media can only be imagined. *This* was news. Jack Ma rode the wave: he was interviewed on CCTV's famous program *Eastern Times*. He was in the headlines, and so was the Internet, which was now gradually becoming hot in China. By 1997 Beijing was sprouting Internet cafes in every alley.

Ma had been successful in getting the *People's Daily* on the Internet and he had done it within six months of first trying. By the day that Web page went up, however, Ma knew that his chances for business success in Beijing were nonexistent. A large group of foreign-invested companies had surged into the market.

With no financial or political backing himself, he could not begin to compete in the country's capital. Never at a loss for ideas, he decided to return to Hangzhou and implement a new stage in his development strategy.

Failure, Success, and the China Yellow Pages

Jack Ma has developed a healthy attitude about failure: he redefines it as success. "Success lies not in how much you have accomplished, but in the fact that you have done something, experienced the process, and begun to learn something."

Ma was to experience this process with his company, the China Yellow Pages. He returned to Hangzhou to find the company in a perilous situation. As the Internet became the focus of acceptable media attention, it spawned dozens of new companies, several of which targeted the space that the Yellow Pages had taken. One of these was the company Yaxin, started by a man named Tian Nining. Yaxin came close to killing off the China Yellow Pages. Ma's fiercest competitor at the time, however, was Hangzhou Telecom, a company with registered capital of almost $36 million (RMB 300 million). Jack Ma, on the other hand, had registered capital of only $2,380 (RMB 20,000). Going up against Hangzhou Telecom was going to be a fight to the finish, and it was quite apparent who was going to win. This was a case of "one mountain cannot have two tigers." In addition to Hangzhou Telecom, Yaxin was biting at Ma's heels. Hangzhou Telecom had extremely strong civic and government backing, while Jack Ma was regarded as a kind of renegade, a guerrilla fighter. He had little credibility, and this diminished even more when the Hangzhou Telecom simply used Chinesepage for its English name, very similar to Ma's

Chinapage. In doing this, it blithely carved away a large part of Ma's market.

In order to save his China Yellow Pages from certain death, Ma decided to "draw close to a large mountain," as the saying goes in Chinese. Everyone knows that when you are attacked, it is best to have a large presence right behind you. Ma decided to work together with Hangzhou Telecom. In March 1996, the assets of China Yellow Pages were converted into $71,500 (RMB 600,000), which constituted 30 percent of shares. Hangzhou Telecom invested $167,000 (RMB 1.4 million), constituting 70 percent of shares. Ma had his mountain, but in the process he relinquished his own company.

The decision to cooperate with Hangzhou Telecom was unavoidable, but before long the partnership ran into problems. The new owner wanted to grow the company fast and also make money fast. Ma's approach was to grow the company slowly and carefully. He felt that you couldn't ask a three-year-old child to go out and make a living. The difference in opinion quickly led to a split, and the partner with the most capital and authority naturally had the most say. The conflict sparked the attention of the *People's Daily*, as well as other media, and the parting of the ways was not comfortable. Ma was asked to stay on by Hangzhou Telecom, but he felt wronged and believed his presence would not be positive. Many staff wanted to leave with Ma, but he insisted that a core group stay on to keep the company going. He transferred his own shares, 21 percent of the company, over to employees and asked them to carry on their good work.

The year 1997 marked Ma's first failure in business. To this day there are many rumors about why he left the company, and he himself is not absolutely certain why he did so. The most likely reason is his strong sense of individuality and individual achievement. He was ready to reach for the next stage.

"Let's Go Home Together"

Since founding the China Yellow Pages, Ma had been forced to deal with countless closed doors. He had grown accustomed to handling negative responses. "You just had to be able to carry on, and in fact each setback made you stronger. I generally assume that something terrible is going to happen tomorrow, and so I prepare for it mentally. When it happens, it doesn't seem so bad. I'm able to deal with it. I begin to say, 'Come on, what else can you do to me?' It gives you self-confidence."

Ma is known for his appreciation of Winston Churchill. He particularly likes Churchill's famous words in his address of 1941: "Never give in—never, never, never, in nothing great or small, large or petty." This became one of Jack Ma's abiding mantras. Another was "Move forward with confidence; surpass your own goals." When he slipped, though, Jack Ma picked himself up and simply started hiking down the road again. After he left China Yellow Pages in 1997, the Ministry of Foreign Economic Relations and Trade (MOFERT) asked him to come join them as an affiliated company in Beijing. He accepted and, together with a core team of his founding members, he began to work on developing trade Web sites for MOFERT in Beijing. From 1998 to 1999 he headed an information technology company established by China International Electronic Commerce Center (CIECC), a department of the Ministry of Foreign Trade and Economic Cooperation (MOFTEC). He rented a twenty-square-meter office where the team worked night and day. The results became the first ministerial-level Web site in China. Ma held 30 percent of shares in this company; the ministry held 70 percent. This meant that Ma drew $300 or $400 dollars a month in salary (a few thousand RMB) and that was about it. The chances of making any money off the shares were nil; meanwhile, the realities of working for the government were unpleasant. Developing a plan and executing it involved too many people and far too many unclear and undefined things. To a man who was not accustomed to being told what to do by others, Ma's role was increasingly awkward. He evaluated his options, which were either to stay in Beijing or to leave. If he stayed, he could join Sina or Yahoo! (both of which were growing in China), but he felt that the Internet activity in Beijing was too hastily done, too impetuous. He knew it would be hard to make anything come of it in the end. Moreover, he was fed up with the halting, erratic nature of progress in the government and the overly cautious approach that made everything fearsome and hard. Ma's intuition told him that the high tide of the Internet around the world was coming fast, and he would miss it if he stayed within the government. He did not want to lose the opportunity of a lifetime, and after long deliberation, he decided to return to Hangzhou.

He called together all the people in his team. They had accompanied him from Hangzhou to Beijing, and they had worked well together. When Ma announced his decision, they were speechless. He then said, "I am giving you three choices. First, you can go to work with Yahoo! I'll recommend you and I know that the company will not only welcome you but the salaries will be high. Second, you can go to work for Sina or Sohu: they'll similarly welcome you and the salaries won't be too bad. Or third, you can come home with me. However, you'll get just $95 [RMB 800] in salary per month, you'll have to rent your own flat and live within a five-minute radius of where I live, since in order to save money I won't allow you to take taxis, and moreover you'll have to work in my home. You make your own decision." He gave them three days to decide.

Everyone in the room filed out. Within three minutes, they filed back in again. Every single person on the team had decided to "come home" with him. Ma had held himself back until that moment, but on hearing this he started to cry. He later described how a hot wave coursed through his body and in that moment he resolved never to let these people down. "All right," he said to himself, "we are going back, starting from zero. And we are going to build a company that we will never have any regrets about for our whole lives."

In the fourteen months that Ma had worked with this team in Beijing, he had never gone on an outing to the countryside with them. They worked all the time. He decided that before leaving the north, they should make an excursion to the Great Wall. Walking along that wall, however, the team felt more of a heavy apprehension about what was to come than any kind of exultation. It was unclear what might be in store for them. Here they had spent more than a year of their lives working like madmen and they had nothing to show for it: they had no savings, no foothold in Beijing, no lasting results.

On the evening before leaving Beijing, the group came together for a final celebratory meal. The wine flowed, the food was excellent, Jack Ma spoke, and eventually somebody started to sing traditional Chinese songs. The first song was "True Blue," and then came others. They avoided a song called "Parting," which was simply too sad to bear. The next day, few could remember what Ma had said, and they had little idea of what they were facing next, but all remembered the song they had first sung together. They remembered that the Shaoxing wine was hot, the emotions were hot, and "True Blue" had been sung with real feeling. Since then, that song has enabled the company team to ride over many rough patches. For example, during the first Internet slump in 2000 and 2001 or during the epidemic of severe acute respiratory syndrome (SARS) in 2003, team members would start to sing and would indeed feel better. The moment an "Ali person" heard the tune, he would remember the old spirit. The song came to represent a belief in the company; it gave people hope.

The departure from Beijing was in 1999, and it marked the

second time that Jack Ma had encountered what he considered a failure. Never one to look backward, he moved on. On the very day that another well-known Internet founder, Ding Lei, brought his company, NetEase, north to Beijing, Jack Ma moved his company and his team south to Hangzhou.

Setbacks

Ma had been through two failures, and he saw no need to be reticent about them. When he spoke of them, however, he was not lighthearted. They had taught him serious lessons. He believed that success is an attitude, a state of mind, and that attitude is a function of individual choice. With your back to the sun, the world is cast in shadows. Ma generally kept his face to the sun.

Lessons learned while in Beijing were to be important to his success with Alibaba. "Before I went to Beijing, I was a small tradesman from Hangzhou," Ma later candidly confessed. "Working for the national government, I learned about the direction of China's future development. I learned to evaluate things from a macro perspective. I was no longer the proverbial frog at the bottom of the well, able to see only a small circle of sky directly above." Ma had participated in the construction of MOFERT's official Web site, and later also China's Web-based product marketplace. He had set up a number of other national-level sites relating to trade. He had learned specific things about how to create sites and how to do business.

His experience with the China Yellow Pages and his departure from Hangzhou Telecom made him realize that if you want to make money on the Internet, you have to be very concrete. Fourteen months in Beijing had given him a sense of China's macroeconomic policy. Working at this level, at the forefront of the

Internet in China, had also allowed him to evaluate the coming wave of the Internet throughout China. He saw that the challenges ahead included, most of all, how to restrain himself and stick to a plan. Jack Ma had been through sufficient ups and downs to look further ahead and see where the next wave would be coming from, how to ride it, how to see the direction of the Internet's greatest potential and hold on long enough to realize it.

By the end of 1998, Ma's thinking about B2B models had matured. His research indicated that the volume of such enterprises on the Internet would be far greater than the volume between businesses and consumers (B2C). The past five years of experience had familiarized him with international trade markets, Chinese domestic producers, and import and export companies, and he saw that the greatest need for e-commerce services and support lay among the thirty million or so small and medium-sized enterprises in China. Ma has said that he believes strategic business decisions rely 60 percent on instinct and 40 percent on statistical analysis and rational evaluation of facts. "What do I want to do?" is often a more important consideration to businessmen than "What can I do?"

In selecting the business of servicing small and medium-sized enterprises, Ma told his team, "I have heard of those who get rich by raising lots of shrimp. I've never heard of those who get rich by catching whales. In the world economy today," he continued, "large corporations are whales. They rely on the smaller fry for their livelihood. Smaller shrimp rely currently on eating the leftovers of the whales, and they also depend on one another. In an Internet-based world, though, we are entering a new business model, where small enterprises can, via the Internet, be independent. A greater diversity of products will be more available to a broader range of customers. Humans are going to be organizing themselves in wholly new ways; the revolutionary nature of the Internet lies in this structural change."

chapter 3

Two Small Enlightenments

Successful entrepreneurs tend to be great students, for they excel at observing and listening. As a result, they are able to mold extraordinary accomplishments out of what others take to be impossible situations. Jack Ma was able to grab on to the lessons of two small satoris and follow them successfully through a kind of baptism of fire. Satoris are, as Webster's defines, "sudden enlightenments leading to a state of consciousness attained by intuitive illumination." The failures in Ma's early period had put him under great pressure. From the Haibo Translation House to the China Yellow Pages to the Ministry of Foreign Economic Relations and Trade, Ma had been buffeted. Rather than be blinded and confused by it, however, he found that the adversity made him more focused, resilient, and determined.

Like so many others in China, he became one of the float-ing population of unemployed. Unlike others, he had no doubts about his future prospects since he and his team were already incubating a huge dream. The first of the two satoris that con-tributed to the dream came before Ma left Beijing, on the day he and his team scaled the Great Wall. In places, the wall has been de-faced by graffiti—names and dates carved into the stone. Ma felt that carving one's name into an ancient cultural monument was a despicable practice, but at the same time it made him wonder why people felt they had to do it. The satori came in recognizing that graffiti on the wall was an embryonic form of bulletin board systems, or BBS, on the Internet. People somehow needed to say, "I'm here too." Capitalizing on this would lead to a broad-based membership for his new business. Relying on a natural human instinct, the energies of the site would come from the people themselves. At an early stage, Ma understood the compounding network effect of interactions among different kinds of people on an Internet site.

The second satori came in February 1999, when Ma at-tended an e-commerce conference held in Singapore. He had made something of a name for himself in Internet circles while at MOFERT, and so he was favored with an invitation to speak at this event. "Favored" is the appropriate word here; although this was a so-called Asian Conference, held in Singapore, in fact more than 80 percent of attendees were Europeans and Americans. In 1999 e-commerce had hardly begun in Asia, yet organizers were sparing no expense in bringing together a group of Westerners who got up onstage to talk with convic-tion about something the Westerners knew little about. Natu-rally, these Westerners drew on their experience with Western e-commerce—eBay, Amazon—while Jack Ma sat in the audience, quietly listening and thinking.

When it came to his turn to speak, he started out, in fluent English, by declaring, "Asian e-commerce is moving in the wrong direction. Asia is Asia. America is America. All e-commerce in the world today follows the American model, but Asia will require its own unique model." Ma generally spoke after deep and prolonged thinking. He has said in the past, "I am absolutely not an impetuous man. I often spend a long time by myself, just thinking." This time, however, his "crazy talk" surprised even himself. Behind the rush of words, however, were fully prepared ideas—in the Chinese phrase, he had the bamboo fully grown in his heart before it sprang forth. Ma's conclusion was that "the revolutionary significance of the Internet is that it will enable small enterprises to operate independently." And Ma wanted to be a savior to China's countless small and medium-sized enterprises.

What exactly did Jack Ma mean by a "unique model" for Asia? Although he spoke for an hour, this is something he did not reveal. Known for being canny, he generally raised questions at conferences but kept his own thinking to himself. This model was something that Ma intended to build into his new business, to create a model that China lacked but that also could not be found in America.

His profound understanding of the business difficulties confronting small enterprises in southern China led to this model. The insight began when he taught English to businessmen at night school and deepened after his exposure to international trade at MOFERT; thus, he approached the Internet business from the perspective of need and sales, not the perspective of technology. One investor dismissed Ma by saying, "The Internet is a high-tech field. People have a lot more faith in a Chinese student who has returned with a Western MBA than they do in a mere English teacher, a graduate of Hangzhou Normal University." Ma knew that he was in many respects far more fortunate than those who had studied abroad, but this sounded like mere hubris, so he kept it to himself.

Once he had succeeded with Alibaba, Ma could explain in speeches, "China business is done here, not over there. So those students who return have to spend a lot of time learning the current situation, whereas I was born and bred here and stayed here, and I was therefore able to see a business opportunity that they all missed."

Unlike many others who engaged in Internet business in China, Ma did not grow up in elite circumstances. He did not graduate from a prestigious college, as Ding Lei had done; he did not go abroad for an education, as Yang Zhiyan had done. He stayed close to the grassroots level in China, and it was for this reason that his e-commerce business model was so different. He decided not to focus on the 15 percent of business that was large corporations but rather the 85 percent that was small and medium-sized enterprises. "I'm going for the small fry," he said. He boiled it down to a very simple equation: large enterprises have their own channels of information and tremendous advertising budgets, while small enterprises have none. Small enterprises are most in need of the Internet—and where there is a need, there is a market. "If you divide enterprises into rich people and poor people, the Internet is a realm for poor people," Ma once explained. "The price for a Web page is basically the same. I want to enable poor people to use this tool to rise in a kind of revolution." Ma knew that he could profit by helping the needy rise.

Jack Ma's homeland province of Zhejiang is one of the hotspots in China for private enterprise. One of the most acute analyses has been done by the journalist Wu Xiaobo, who spent years researching Wenzhou trading networks. Thousands of small enterprises contend for business in the region. Through exposure to the most basic levels of market making, Jack Ma was familiar with the difficulties these enterprises faced. "For example, take Wal-Mart. Wal-Mart can force a supplier to accept a low price because it is making orders in the tens of millions. A supplier has no way out but to accept. The next year, though, Wal-Mart has an auction among suppliers for the same product and somebody *else* gets the order. The first guy is washed up. He has no fallback, he has no marketing arm. If he goes through the Internet, on the other hand, he can look all over the world on a global scale for customers and keep a customer base of his own. He also gets to keep far more of his margin." The proletariat had been called to arise and liberate themselves in the past, but now Jack Ma wanted the countless small enterprises of his homeland to liberate themselves.

With his idealism came a good measure of business savvy. "Asia is the largest supplier base in the world for exports," he said. "Among the great density of small companies here, most do not have channels to the large trading companies. Most have no way to reach a market. Simply by going through our Alibaba network, they can get access to all of America and Europe." Again, Ma's mantra: where there is a need, there is a market.

In order to put some numbers to his business savvy, in 2008 there were about 32 million small and medium-sized enterprises in China. Of these, 2.6 million were regularly conducting import/export trading. In 2007 around 8.8 million of all small enterprises in China used online B2B services for domestic or international trade. Small enterprises spent an average of 11 percent of their marketing budget online. By providing this segment with online services that range from credit checks and banking facilities to advertising and marketing, Ma leveraged his small company into a major force.

Alibaba's Founding Declaration

Small and medium-sized enterprises are like grains of sand on a beach. The Internet can glue them together. It can make them into an invincible force that is able to go up against the big stones. The virtue of the Internet is that it uses small to compete with big, it uses fast to compete with slow.

—JACK MA

In February 1999, Alibaba began its life quietly in the small residential area of Lakeside Garden, Hangzhou. There was no sign on the door, no indication of any activity. All was simple and unpretentious and anonymous, as Jack Ma wanted it to be. His reasons for choosing Hangzhou were simple. "Hangzhou was far from the IT centers in Beijing and Shenzhen, and the cost of human talent was cheap." In addition, Ma stuck to his earliest principles, which were formed through an understanding, to the point of infatuation, with what is known in Chinese martial arts novels as "rivers and lakes," the mythical equivalent of Robin Hood's Sherwood Forest. It is interesting to note how similar the legendary heroes were: Robin Hood and his Merry Men are said to have lived in the thirteenth century, and many of the stories of Ma's favorite book, *Outlaws of the Marsh*, date from the twelfth and thirteenth centuries. The term is infused with the idea of a brotherhood of Robin Hood–style outlaws: those who take from the rich and give to the poor.

As soon as Ma arrived in Hangzhou, he called a meeting of his team to start the new campaign. He made sure that this first comprehensive meeting of the company was recorded on videotape because he firmly believed that it would be regarded as historic in the future. The tape is excellent documentary footage. Eighteen people sit and stand around in subdued lighting, looking very serious, while Jack Ma talks in a hyperanimated fashion. "It is darkest before dawn," he declares. "So we grope together through the darkness. We call to each other. And when I say 'Charge!' we do it without fear or panic. We carry a big axe and we charge together, for if two dozen of us charge at the same time, what is there to be afraid of?" In this first meeting, the company gathered together its first financial resources. Ma asked everyone to pitch in from their own coffers—he strictly forbade anyone to borrow money from family or friends. The possibility of failure was not insignificant. "If the winds of Taishan [Mountain] blow us over, though, I will just be getting up and starting the struggle again."

Everyone dug deep, and the result was some $60,000 (RMB 500,000) in initial investment. Ma laid down three rules: no one would have high compensation, no one would have a high position, and everybody would be in this together. "I was really talking like a madman that day," recalls Ma, his face breaking into a smile at the memory. "I told them all, 'Put your money out here on the table.' In the end, we pulled together $60,000, not too bad. That was our first invested capital. I also made sure they realized there was only one path before them—there was no going back. If we failed, at least we would have been considered honorable."

Blessed with the gift of motivating people, Ma could not let this historic occasion pass without making a speech. "We aim to create an e-commerce company, and in doing this we have three specific goals. First, we want to set up a company that lasts for one hundred and two years. Second, we want to establish a company that provides e-commerce services to China's small and medium-sized companies. Third, we want to set up the world's largest e-commerce company, one that will enter the ranks of the top ten names among global Internet sites."

More than nine years have passed since then, during which time the Internet worldwide went through the end of the dot-com bubble (what is known in China as the "bitterly cold winter") and then began to be accepted as a normal and necessary part of life. All eighteen founding members resolutely stayed in their positions at Alibaba throughout. What's more, these "young upstarts" have become the core backbone of the company.

During the course of the founding meeting at Ma's apartment in Hangzhou, the walls suddenly began oozing water from a leak upstairs. He told everyone to hold tight as he went out to get "material." Back in a minute, his arms were full of newspapers. All the founding members pitched in and helped plaster the news-papers against the walls, then carried on with the meeting as if nothing had happened. It is said that later, in order to keep the décor looking unified, Ma decorated the whole room with this newspaper "wallpaper."

Alibaba Is Born

To the Chinese way of thinking, one always wants to keep one's cutting edge out of sight. In fact, one wants to make sure it is deeply hidden. This philosophy extends to official presentation of the news: the hard edge of tough editorials is softened by putting a human-interest story nearby. Tools are manufactured with an acute sharpness, and one always wants to file that down a little be-fore using them. Being a man also has its sharpness, although the usual way of expressing this in Chinese is to call it a man's "line." The ancient saying goes, "The most accomplished are those who keep their cutting edge concealed, for only then can a man reach the ideal state of being." This was an adage well used in the early days by Jack Ma.

During the preparatory period of Alibaba, the usually strident Jack Ma was as silent as a rabbit. He kept his edge hidden. Soft, quiet, he disappeared from public view. He worked all day and night from his home, in rooms that sometimes had as many as thirty-five people working together. Resources were limited, but nobody cared. Ma continued motivating his team. "When you hear the sound of the starting gun," he would tell them, "you don't have time to look around and see how your opponent is doing. You just have to run like hell." Then he would warn them, "Your greatest enemy is yourself; your greatest opponent is time. And your greatest failure is to give up." The group worked hard—often sixteen to eighteen hours a day—designing and programming Web pages 24/7. Neighbors probably thought the hours of these young people somewhat strange, but they waited and watched to see what the result might be.

In March 1999, the Alibaba Web site was officially released. "When the naming is right," as the Chinese saying goes, "words flow properly. First one must get the title right." Authors and journalists alike know that is half the battle, and Jack Ma showed considerable foresight in naming his company Alibaba. He knew that the company would eventually be international, and that it should have a name that was resonant in all languages and could be understood over the world. He thought for a long time about this name, testing it in various venues. For example, while eating dinner in the United States, he asked the waiter if he had heard of Ali Baba. "Sure, and the secret code for opening up the treasure trove is 'Open Sesame.'" People all over the world seemed to know the name and the story. He decided that the company had to be called Alibaba.

Unfortunately, the domain name had already been registered in Canada. Despite the paucity of funds, Ma spent $10,000 to buy back the domain name. Few could understand his extravagance at the time, and attributed it to a lifelong sense of idealism. Ma's action was far better done then, however, than later: in April

2004, Google spent over $1 million to buy the domain names google.com.cn and google.cn. This was the highest price ever paid at that time for a .cn domain name transaction. The two domain names had been snatched early on by the Beijing National Network Company. In order to get them, Google appealed to the China International Economics and Trade Arbitration Commission, but the suit was rejected; Google then decided to spend the money and purchase the names. The incident was highly effective in raising investors' awareness of the importance of domain names.

Being Coy: Attracting the Media with Silence

Jack Ma is known as an outstanding businessman, but few recognize that he is also highly adept at working the media: he is familiar with how the system works. Conservative when it comes to promotion strategies, he does in fact have a highly developed sense of smell when it comes to news. Alibaba's uncommon reticence was very effective in spurring the media to great curiosity. In May 1999, a Hangzhou publication put out an article called "Alibaba Refuses Visitors, While Wanting to Be a Global Trade Marketplace." This coy attitude only whetted the appetite of the press. Soon overseas media began to show interest as well. The first to come to Hangzhou was the magazine *BusinessWeek*. Shortly after that, the *South China Morning Post* came calling.

The journalist from *BusinessWeek* finally found Alibaba's offices in the small Lakeside residential district. When he walked in, he was reportedly shocked into silence. He later described the working conditions as being a tiny space holding some twenty people, with sheets and bedding strewn about the floor and an odor that was something akin to old shoes. Despite primitive conditions, the company's work was impressive. It involved listing products of manufacturing and trading companies on a Web site.

Soon Alibaba's—and Jack Ma's—reputation was growing by the day in Europe and America. The hit rate from overseas began to increase, and the number of members in what was called the Alibaba Club at that time rose explosively. Without spending one penny, Jack Ma had attracted the international media attention that others were trying so hard to get. Zhang Chaoyang at Sohu in the early days appeared on talk shows, which seemed to give some people a negative impression: if Zhang Chaoyang could spend so much time on television, how could he be effective in running a company? He explained his reasons in 2003: "Sohu is a portal. It needs traffic. But since I didn't have money back then, I had to go on the road myself. It's not like today when we ask movie stars to be our spokesmen." This lament had some logic to it, but Ma's ability to play the media worked better. He attributed it to his early years in setting up the China Yellow Pages and then the time he spent fraternizing with media and journalists in Beijing.

Financing

Competition is like mobile warfare. Winning and losing are determined by the speed of your reactions both to the future market and to the need for capital.

—Jack Welch, former CEO, General Electric

No matter how attractive to the media the proselytizer Jack Ma might have become, venture capitalists still knew that Alibaba had not in fact made any money. They knew, moreover, that it sorely lacked funds. Dot-com companies were famously good at burning money, and Alibaba was no exception. Large operating expenses ate up capital, making it hard for Ma to catch his breath. Fortunately, his global speaking appearances served two purposes: they drew in customers, and they drew in venture capital.

In opening up the virgin territory of e-commerce, the fact that one needed both a market and also capital was brutally apparent: only by occupying a market and also having sufficient funding could Ma and Alibaba hope to succeed. By the end of 1999, money had become the company's greatest problem. Since the scalable effect of the Internet is greater than any other economic form, its thirst for capital is also greatest. By July 1999, Alibaba's strained circumstances were already forcing Ma to "borrow" by deducting money from employee salaries.

Strangely enough, the Russian AK-47 assault rifle inadvertently came to Alibaba's rescue. The AK-47s in question appeared on Alibaba's Web site, apparently unbeknownst to the company. Someone had put in an offer to sell them on the site, which attracted the attention of *Business Week*. This news was a great shock to Jack Ma. His staff searched the Web site but could find no mention of the item. As Ma remembers, "It really was hardly possible. I knew that the most important issue on the Internet was credibility and trust, so from the beginning I established the rule that every bit of information put on our Web site had to be monitored and approved by a staff member. We have followed that rule from the time we had free membership all the way down to today. Because of that, I believe this kind of information could not have appeared on Alibaba. For the news to appear in *Business Week* scared me, however, since that is a publication that is not careless about what it says." The story affected Alibaba negatively to a minute degree, but it also brought with it considerable international attention. Trotting along with the media attention came the attention of foreign investors.

No Begging

Soon Ma was faced with an army of venture capitalists. Although in need of funding, he claims he was not seduced by their money. Most of them were domestic companies or individuals, wanting terms that he considered extortionist. Others did not bring enough lateral resources to the table. A well-known journalist for *Caijing Magazine*, Zheng Zuoshi, notes the following story in his record of a meeting with Alibaba's former deputy CFO, Peng Lei:

Ma received a phone call while he was at his house at Lakeside Garden one day in July 1999. He looked over the people in the company who were there at the time, and then said to Peng Lei, "Would you come out with me for a while?"

Peng Lei went down with him, only to learn that they would be attending a meeting with a potential investor. She had not prepared and had brought along nothing but a notepad: no statistics, no documentation. Jack, for his part, had brought nothing at all.

Peng Lei does not remember the name of the venture capitalist by now. All she remembers is that they met with the manager of the Shanghai office of an international investment firm. Three people had come from Shanghai and were staying at the World Trade Hotel in Hangzhou. They had already visited Alibaba's offices at Lakeside, and they knew what Alibaba did. They had the power in their own hands to make a decision within the scope of a certain level of investment. This negotiation with Jack Ma was therefore quite concrete. If they came to an agreement, the money would be forthcoming.

Five people attended. Peng Lei and a man from the venture capital firm sat on the sofa. Ma sat on a bed, but as usual he soon got up and strode back and forth. One of the others sat on another bed; the first sat on a stool at the small writing table. After introductory formalities the talk moved into specifics. The investor raised a figure and a specific ownership percentage. He reiterated that if Ma agreed, they could make the decision themselves. Ma did not seem happy with the share percentage, however; the dollar amount being discussed was in the range of $1 million. The negotiations stalled when Ma indicated that the money being offered was insufficient to justify the percentage of shares being requested. Ma recommended a short break and said that he and Peng Lei were going outside.

The two left and walked out into the sunny street. After a long period of silence, Ma suddenly asked, "What do you think?" Peng Lei later confessed that she knew this question was rhetorical; in fact, "Ma was not asking for my opinion. He had his own ideas. The question was just to soften the atmosphere of grim silence as we walked along. But at the same time, I knew that Alibaba had no money, since I was in charge of that aspect of the company. I really wanted him to give a little in the negotiation. So I said, 'Ma Yun, there's no money in our account.'"

He didn't make a sound. He walked a little farther, and then said, "Okay, let's go back." Back in the room, Ma told the venture capitalist, "We feel that the total valuation of Alibaba is higher than you feel it is. The distance between us is too great. I'm afraid there is no way we can cooperate." And that concluded the negotiation. Peng Lei still remembers that one of the investors accompanied them down in the elevator. "You are making a big mistake," he told them, "You're passing up a great opportunity."

Why was Alibaba so fastidious with regard to venture capital? Ma explains it by saying that he wanted Alibaba's first infusion of capital to bring with it more than just money. He needed non-financial elements, such as access to overseas resources, as much as he needed raw funds. Because of this, it is said that Jack Ma turned away thirty-eight potential investors in the early years.

Money continued to be scarce. The hard days were not altogether a bad thing, though, for Ma believes it helped in forming a kind of corporate culture, a consciousness of "who we are," and a sense of values that kept the company intact as a team after Alibaba had become powerful. This cohesive corporate culture may increasingly be a nostalgic memory. As Morgan Stanley and others have noted in 2008, "Rapid expansion [of the company] may lead to culture dilution."

Angel Funding from Goldman Sachs

The superheated atmosphere of the Chinese Internet in 1999 attracted the attention of many international investment banks and venture capital companies. They invested serious amounts of money in the Chinese Internet market. Goldman Sachs, Morgan Stanley, and Softbank were three of the primary leads, buying into portals and also into e-commerce.

Sina and Sohu were two main beneficiaries of this investment. Sina is said to have received $16 million in one round of financing in 1999. Sohu took in two rounds of investment, one for $6 million and the other for $30 million. Less than two years later, the three large Internet portals of China were listed on Nasdaq, and investors were able to reap their rewards.

Ma did not let this hot environment go to his head. Together with Cai Chongxin, who had previously served as a senior manager in the venture capital business, he looked carefully for the right investor. In August 1999, Cai became reacquainted with an old friend, and their serendipitous meeting brought Alibaba its first "angel funding." That old friend, a Ms. Lin, had met Cai Chongxin when Cai was still studying at Harvard. By chance, they took the same flight from the United States to Taiwan, and after that initial meeting Cai maintained contact with her due to their common profession. By 1999 Lin was working at Goldman Sachs in the Hong Kong territory as an investment manager. When they met again in 1999, Cai learned that Goldman was looking into Internet funding in China and indeed was planning to take some major action.

Goldman Sachs had previously looked only at traditional industries in China and had little experience in high-tech investing there, so Cai did not harbor great hopes. As a result of Lin's recommendation, however, Goldman Sachs sent a man to Alibaba to look it over. The results were relatively satisfactory, and both Ma and Cai began to feel heavy weights drop from their shoulders. They had rejected suitors they felt were not appropriate, but Goldman Sachs was a different story.

"To tell the truth, Alibaba had little room to maneuver at the time," Cai Chongxin said. "The Internet was hot, but not having any money at all was a huge problem. We had no leeway in haggling over price. Later, when we went for a second round of funding, the situation was different: we could bargain. Goldman's early demands were even more stringent than those of other investors, but after Ma Yun and I talked it over, we decided to take Goldman's money. On the one hand, this was a famous American investment bank and could be useful in opening the American market in the future. On the other hand, Goldman was a sizable company and able to look much farther down the road [in terms of when they needed a return on the investment]. We probably talked it over for ten minutes. Then the thing was decided."

Cai's description shows how hard up Alibaba was at the time, but it also shows how Ma valued the Goldman Sachs brand name. Ma was focused on the rainmaking ability of Goldman Sachs and its ability to attract a market. These were key considerations later when Ma went for more financing. Ma had failed math twice in his youth, but with regard to financing his mind was sharp. He understood the consequences of losing controlling interest, and he knew the potential problems behind his own ownership of control shares. Ma's attitude with regard to money was indeed calculating; he had total respect for the importance of the issue. He did not want large numbers of shares in the hands of any single investor, for who knew what unacceptable situation that investor might force Ma into in the future? At the same time, Ma felt that being the controlling shareholder himself was not as effective as having employees derive benefit from shareholding. All of Alibaba's employees were Ma's friends and had been through hard times together. He believed the saying about "sharing good times as well as bad times, benefits as well as troubles."

As lead investor in a group of investment banks, Goldman invested $5 million in Alibaba in October 1999, becoming not just the first in the initial round of angel investors but also stirring up a tremendous amount of publicity for the small company. A crisis had been averted, and now the company was in good shape and ready to implement its grand plan for the future.

Masayoshi Son Takes a Liking to Alibaba

After this infusion of capital, Alibaba found a new home. Its new office address was 47 China Star Science and Technology Building, third floor, on Wensan Road in Hangzhou. Jack Ma had led Alibaba silently through 1999, but now, with the nourishment of the Goldman Sachs funding, the company grew quickly. By mid-2000, the company was maintaining an excellent growth curve and was well prepared to meet the demands of additional investment. Alibaba had sought a second round of financing immediately after the first, and this time Ma was more at ease in the process.

The prospective investor was the legendary IT kingpin, Masayoshi Son. In the Asian investment world, Son's name is considered to be as famous as that of the NBA's Michael Jordan. Son and Ma are both short in stature, and both have an instinctive intelligence about business. Ma likes to do business with intelligent people; he says that you don't need to say much to be quickly understood. Masayoshi Son was the right kind of person.

Masayoshi Son is of Korean cultural heritage but was born and raised in Japan. It is said that his family originally came to Korea from China and that his genealogy from generations past includes high officials in China's diplomatic service. Family circumstances declined, however, and Son's grandfather immigrated to Japan to work as a laborer in the coal mines on the southern island of Kyushu. Son's personal experiences in childhood were harsh; there are stories about rifling through trash with his grandmother to get food, and the experience is said to have seared into him a fierce determination. His father encouraged him at every stage with the firm belief that he was a genius. He attributed his phenomenal success primarily to self-confidence.

Son did well in school, and in 1973 his parents sent him for a brief course in English in San Francisco. The courses were taught through a religious institution, and he stayed with relatives in southern San Francisco. At one point on this first visit, he visited the University of California at Berkeley, where he was exposed to free thinkers and optimists, who were legion there at the time. This method of thinking was absent in regimented, discriminatory Japan, and Son determined to return to Berkeley as soon as he could as a college student.

Son had already decided to focus on computers as his core interest. When he got to Berkeley, he took economics and computer courses, and he began to develop his entrepreneurial instincts. He even patented a device that eventually sold to Sharp Electronics for $1 million. With this investment, he imported video arcade games to Berkeley and placed them around the campus, which generated excellent cash flow.

He had made his first million U.S. dollars by the time he was twenty. He graduated from college at the age of twenty-one, sold his company, and returned to Japan. By the age of forty-three, before the dot-com bubble burst, Son was considered the richest man in Asia. He could single-handedly move shares on the Japanese market. Any meeting between Jack Ma and this legendary figure was bound to be a historic event. The early bond between these two may well have come from recognizing that both had been social outcasts as children.

This first meeting in late November 1999 was orchestrated by Morgan Stanley, under the guidance of a man named Sunil Gupta. Gupta had called Ma in early autumn 1999 to ask him about Alibaba's general financial situation. Four weeks later, Ma received an e-mail from Gupta, telling him that "a person wants to have a confidential meeting with you, and I believe he will be an extremely useful person for you to know."

Goldman Sachs' first round of financing had just been completed on November 30, 1999, so on the next day Jack Ma, in high spirits and with a lofty degree of confidence, headed to this so-called confidential meeting with an unknown person. The meeting turned out to be quite different from what Ma expected. First, he had not expected to be meeting Softbank's legendary founder Masayoshi Son. Second, he had not expected that the meeting would be open to many others, including such heavy hitters in China's Internet world as Wang Zhidong, Zhang Chaoyang, and Ding Lei. Ma was a relatively small figure in such company.

Since so many people had shown up to present investment opportunities to him, Masayoshi Son could only meet with each for twenty minutes. When Jack Ma's turn came, he stood up and spent a few minutes explaining his company—what it did and what it planned to do. "Son was extremely smart," Ma later recalled. "He understood everything after I'd said only a few words. He had a keen intuitive sense and a quick understanding. Moreover, his character was pretty similar to mine—we both said things like 'I want this, I want that.'" Ma spoke for a mere six minutes before being stopped by Son, who indicated that he had a strong interest in investing. He asked Ma how much money he needed. Ma's response to this legendary investor was shocking: he told Son he didn't need money. "If you don't need money, why did you come looking for me?" Son asked. Ma responded somewhat like a petulant child: he not come looking but had been asked to come by others.

The conversation seems comic now, but the truly funny thing was what came later. Although Ma had just received $5 million in investment, in those wild days of Internet investing, $5 million was nothing. Ma now says he really did feel that he was not in need of money. Nobody knows if he was just saying this to draw attention to his uniqueness among all the hungry others or if he really meant it. One thing is certain: Jack Ma knew how to handle investors. He believed that all investors were basically the same: if you make money, they try to give you more. If you don't make money and have to go begging for it, they turn and run. A chased investor can run like a rabbit. Now, Ma's avowed lack of any need for money stimulated Son's interest. Just before leaving, he invited Jack to come to Japan for detailed discussions.

Twenty days after this first meeting, Jack Ma visited Masayoshi Son in Tokyo along with his finance director, Cai Chongxin. The first thing out of Son's mouth was, "We want to invest in you, and we want to hold 30 percent of shares." The machine-gun style did not faze Ma at all, nor did the lightning-fast decisions. Ma considered this offer of a $30 million investment in return for 30 percent of shares for five or six minutes before beginning to nod. Cai Chongxin held a different view, however, and said no. This was later to become a rather famous no in Internet circles.

Cai described the scene as follows. "First, you have to have courage to say no to Masayoshi Son. He is the kind of person who doesn't take no for an answer. In the Internet world at the time, his investment in Yahoo! Japan was already famous, it was talked about so much it was, as they say, putting calluses on people's ears. I said no to him three times, probably because our funding was relatively adequate at the time. The first time was when he named a price. I said no immediately without even thinking about it. Moreover, I said it quite firmly. I told him that we could reject the offer without going through the board of directors. We simply could not accept it."

A large calculator sat in front of Masayoshi Son. After this first refusal, he calculated for a minute on this machine and then announced another price. Cai said that he, Jack Ma, and Alibaba could not accept this price either for the number of shares. So Son again addressed his calculator. After a moment, he came up with another price, which was also refused. Finally Son's terms came within a range that both Ma and Cai Chongxin could accept. The two sides came to an agreement: the sum of financing would remain at $30 million with share percentages that were acceptable to both sides.

In details that were later divulged by Cai Chongxin, we learn that the negotiation was tough. And yet when Ma came back to China, he began to have second thoughts. Never greedy, he now felt that the money was not too little but rather too much. Ma called Son's assistant and told him, "We only want as much money as we need, and that is $20 million. Too much money is a bad thing." Son's assistant could hardly believe this desire to turn away money—nobody had ever told Son that he was investing too much.

Ma sent Son an e-mail to clarify the situation. "I hope to join hands with Mr. Masayoshi Son and enter the Internet together . . . [but] if our cooperation was not meant to be, then we should still be good friends." Five minutes later, Jack Ma received a response from Son. "Thank you for giving me a business opportunity. We will definitely help to put Alibaba's name out in the world, help it become an Internet site on the level of Yahoo!" Son agreed to Ma's suggestion: a Softbank investment of $20 million, with Alibaba's management team still holding a controlling number of shares. Cai Chongxin later noted that forgoing a large percentage of shares was the biggest concession Son had ever made in his whole history of investing.

Why not take money that was offered to him? Ma has said, looking back, "Yes, I was gambling, but I only gamble on things over which I have control. Our team was still less than sixty people—I had at most $20 million to spend, but I could have done it with $2 million. More than $20 million was superfluous. It lost its value. It would be detrimental to the enterprise, so I had to go back on my word and refuse it."

Outstanding entrepreneurs appear to make investment decisions in the millions without batting an eye, while at the same time they save every penny they can. Only if one has respect for the value of money can any investment achieve its highest value. Many ask if this strange story is really true. Jack Ma has publicly stated as much on a CCTV program. He added, "No matter what you are doing, material gain should not be your main motivation. When all a person is thinking about is money, all he has in his mind are RMB, HK dollars, U.S. dollars, it involuntarily comes out in his speech. Then nobody is willing to cooperate with him. People hear it, and they shun the person."

Ma felt that he and Masayoshi Son were similar kinds of people. "Son hides his intelligence under seeming ignorance. He has an impassive face. He speaks garbled English, but there is not one superfluous word in what he says. He is like a kind of martial arts master. In those six minutes in which we initially met, we understood what kind of person the other was. First, we are people who are fast at making decisions. Second, we are men who want to accomplish major things. Third, we want to realize our own way of thinking." He later added, "I believe that investors like me, and Masayoshi Son likes me, simply because I tell them quite honestly what I am going to accomplish and how much money it is going to make. Son saw my spirit. There are many people in the world who have a lot of money, but there aren't many who can make something out of Alibaba. I think that this is where our self-confidence comes from. If investors don't give us money, we can get it elsewhere. I only go to those who are willing and happy to participate. There are many investors in the world, but there is only one Jack Ma. That's the way it is."

Injecting an additional $20 million into the company at that time was not necessarily the wisest course of action. Alibaba had just received an infusion from the Goldman Sachs team, and its reputation was soon to increase mightily as a result. Waiting a little for another round of financing would have allowed the company to value itself more highly and would have allowed it to relinquish fewer shares. Nonetheless, as events later proved, the timing could not have been better. In April 2000, the Nasdaq began a prolonged two-year decline. After April, no China Internet company could find any funding at all. On the other hand, Alibaba and Jack Ma had plenty of grass to eat through this lean period and never had to worry about a roof over their heads.

The Largest Private Offering in the History of China's Internet

By 2004 Alibaba was considered to be the world's largest B2B e-commerce Web site. On February 17, 2004, Alibaba announced in Beijing that it would be raising the large sum of $82 million in strategic investment. This was the largest private offering up to that time in the history of China's Internet. The investors included Softbank, Fidelity Fund Investment Group, Granite Global Ventures (GGV), and the venture capital firm TDF.

Softbank, Fidelity, and TDF had already invested in Alibaba over the past four years. GGV, headquartered in Silicon Valley, was a newcomer. Softbank led this private offering, after which it continued to be the second-largest shareholder of Alibaba. Alibaba's largest block of shareholders continued to be the management team of the company and employees. At the time of the investment, Son declared, "We are delighted to have drawn investors in to help Alibaba consolidate its position in this field. The investment is in line with Softbank's strategic policy of finding companies that can occupy leading positions in their markets." Ma accepted the financing in part because he felt that the Internet in China would soon be going through a structural change. He foresaw a new group of Internet users, namely "Net businesses," taking over the dominant role from user groups that were typically called "Net people" (those who accessed the Internet for the main purpose of sending e-mails, reading news, and looking up information) and "Net friends" (those who used the Internet mostly for short messages, instant messaging, game playing, and dating). Ma felt that information gathering, social networking, and e-mailing functions were going to give way to "Net business" as the dominant use of the Internet, and he wanted to be positioned to benefit from this change. A cartoon at the time showed him thin and gaunt as ever, dressed in Arab attire, with his mouth wide open in a naive and innocent smile. One hand grasped a huge bag while the other stuffed fistfuls of money into it.

In fact, this cartoon was not far from reality. Alibaba's business had been growing steadily in the B2B realm. At the end of 2000, so-called Alibaba Club members were increasing at the rate of one thousand to two thousand per day. Every day, some thirty-five hundred lines of product information were being received from suppliers and buyers. More than seven hundred types of product information were by now categorized by type of product and national origin. An American who wanted to buy, say, a thousand badminton rackets could find at least a dozen Chinese suppliers on Alibaba. He could view their pricing and their contractual terms. A supplier based in Tibet and a buyer based in Ghana could come together on Alibaba's Web site to do a deal.

By December 27, 2001, the number of members in Alibaba's China Supplier Club had topped one million, making Alibaba the largest B2B Web site in the world in terms of membership. The company showed a profit for the first time that same month. This was a critical moment for Jack Ma, for it began to lend credence to his idea that B2B e-commerce could indeed be profitable.

A tremendous wave of imitators and competitors soon sprang up in China. Some used direct copies of the Alibaba Web site, down to the line about "getting in touch with Alibaba"—the competitor had forgotten to delete or change the name and contact information. The imitators became the source of much merriment as well as distress in the company. Jack Ma had struggled six years for this day. His abiding mantras had included the maxim about being able to bend like bamboo: "If you are too rigid, you are easily broken. Those who know how to bend cannot be defeated." Knowing when to bend and when to fight was the question.

Despite competitors, things began to get easier after this break-even turning point in 2001. Ma began to go on global campaigns, visiting dozens of countries, proselytizing for e-commerce. He also began to put together ideas for what was now an expanded vision of the role of Alibaba. "When businessmen open up their computers today, they see Windows. Everything is Windows. In the future, what we hope you will see is a full-service window of Alibaba. Alibaba will become synonymous with trade."

TrustPass

The company now undertook an initiative called TrustPass in order to facilitate its expanded vision. A way for businesses to rank the trustworthiness of partners, the TrustPass service authenticates and verifies documentation on an enterprise; it requires registration and various types of vetting. This service was marked by a little symbol that first appeared on the Alibaba Web site in March 2002. The TrustPass certificate was an important step in publicizing the value-added services provided by Alibaba.

By 2003, Alibaba was putting out trade software for small and medium-sized enterprises as well, specifically for use in commerce. Both TrustPass and the software called TradePass greatly enhanced the likelihood of successfully completing an online business deal. Most features of the system were aimed at internal trade within China. They used third-party corroboration to give objective evaluations of members. They tallied up the actual record of transactions accomplished on the Alibaba system, helping members understand the business volume and reliability of any given supplier.

Alibaba recognized that a full package of value-added services was the way to prosper from its e-commerce B2B Web site. As a result, it began to offer a range of online and offline services. Online services included third-party verification and authentication, provision of the TrustPass certificate, browsing functions that offered information on hundreds of thousands of buyers, and promotion services for suppliers (including inclusion in keyword searches, management information, immediate buyer feedback, and the ability to be first in line when information on a particular product was requested). Finally, one key benefit in the process was the ability to use Alibaba's unique payment system, known as Alipay. Launched in October 2003, Alipay provided a secure payment platform for both parties in any transaction. Offline services included all kinds of things that might help an enterprise deal with the outside world, particularly an enterprise that was not familiar with international trade. These included training sessions, purchasing negotiations, meetings and conferences at trade shows, and all manner of consulting and professional services.

As part of its initiative to provide value-added services that would turn the Internet into a trade tool, Alibaba began heavily promoting the TradePass software. TradePass was developed as a custom tool to increase the ease of doing business, and it was constantly upgraded to make it more user-friendly and to accommodate suggestions made by businessmen. It combined trade services with online English translation and consolidated customer-management software that allowed businesses to keep track of information on their clients. On June 6, 2006, the software was selected as one of China's top ten software programs due primarily to its usefulness to small and medium-sized enterprises inside China.

In presenting the award for TradePass, the organizers of the event noted, "TradePass has provided us with a bridge for communicating, in all spheres including government, trade, and business. This award is the result of the hard work of those who developed the software. We hope it will encourage others in the software industry in China to put their efforts into developing the growth of China-made software." The very fact of the award made it clear that China-made software was receiving strong support from the government and was uniquely suited to China's needs in the official view. Alibaba appears to be well positioned to grow in this direction.

International TrustPass membership was launched to serve exporters outside China in August 2001. China TrustPass membership was launched to serve small and medium-sized enterprises engaging in domestic trade inside China in March 2002. Both soon generated a new wave of activity on Alibaba. Among its benefits to those wanting to do e-commerce: (1) TrustPass gave buyers a place in which to find sellers. TrustPass members could post photographs of products and information on products, ensuring visibility in Alibaba's vast marketplace. TrustPass members could receive preferential information about buyers' inquiries, could contact customers for free via the service, and could use customer management tools. (2) TrustPass provided authentication of customer information. This allowed buyers to purchase with greater security. (3) Members of TrustPass were able to make use of the Alipay online payment system, which served as a kind of escrow account or guarantor for financial exchanges.

A New Age of E-Commerce: Net Business

Jack Ma has long believed the Internet is transitioning from being an information gathering and social networking tool to becoming first and foremost a venue for online business. Concurrent with this development has been the growth of a new group of Internet users. In order to service this group, Ma proposed back in 2000 that Alibaba create a subset of members, with special privileges, to be called China Suppliers. The term was first presented in such a quiet and unassuming way that many later mixed it up with the TrustPass program.

The term "China Suppliers" refers to a specific project initiated by Ma, namely, the Gold Supplier membership launched to serve China exporters in October 2000. At the same time, the term indicates something broader, something that could be called a general movement in China's Internet usage. Since the concept started in Alibaba's early years, the ever-cautious Ma was careful not to publicize it. His strategy, as in the old days of guerrilla warfare, was to "stealthily enter the village, without any gunfire."

China Suppliers were, in a sense, both customers and the foundation of the so-called Alibaba ecosystem. Ma realized that an entire system had to be created to help those who most needed the Internet. He called this an ecosystem because it was the soil and sustenance for small and medium-sized enterprises that would allow them to grow into being global suppliers.

In recent years, China has become the world's production center. The country has indisputably become the leading supplier of products to the world. The Alibaba system has both enhanced this growth and been a beneficiary of it. Part of this is due to its geographic location in Zhejiang province. Within China, the most vibrant part of the private economy, as represented especially by small and medium-sized enterprises, has centered around the southern provinces, most particularly Zhejiang and Jiangsu.

As more multinationals source their goods from China, "made in China" has become a kind of global event. And yet for smaller producers in Zhejiang and elsewhere in China, reaching foreign buyers remains problematic. Information does not communicate well across the language barrier. Small companies lack the resources to attend the trade fairs in Canton or elsewhere. From the beginning, Ma's China Suppliers program hoped to resolve information flow problems and procedures and thus give small firms more opportunities to reach a marketplace. The content of the China Suppliers program specifically included helping suppliers display their products and company information on the Internet. It included first still images and later video display, creating a unified search channel for customers to find Alibaba's suppliers, and providing suppliers with advice and guidance on basic rules and etiquette in dealing with foreign buyers. There are now more than twenty-two thousand China Suppliers on the Alibaba site. The fee for being a member of the China Suppliers Club is between $5,120 and $15,400 (RMB 40,000–120,000). The numbers bring in revenue: 20,000 suppliers at $5,120 (the minimum fee) is equal to over $100 million. At the maximum fee, the figure is three times higher.

This has vindicated Jack Ma's belief not only that the Internet is a viable tool for business but also that focusing on the small suppliers that make up 85 percent of business is a profitable business model. It has furthermore reinforced his belief that the Internet in general is moving into a new era. As mentioned earlier, the use of Internet has changed over the years in China, with the predominant users of the Internet being classified first as "Net people," then "Net friends," and finally now "Net business." During the "Net people" and "Net friends" phases, profits were made mainly by ISPs; people who accessed the Internet were basically playing the role of consumers, and the profits for Internet companies came from advertising and short messaging. Until 2004 the Internet was still a passive tool with regard to doing business. That has all changed, and now the Internet in China has increasingly been used as an active tool for business. A new business model has arisen that in China is known as "Net business," using the tool of Internet-based e-commerce to conduct commercial activities.

"Net business" also includes a new group of Internet users who are using business applications on the Internet. Ma believes that as this concept becomes more familiar, it will gradually replace the older concepts of "Net people" and "Net friends" in China. Using business applications on the Internet will become an indispensable part of business. In China, as elsewhere, this is generally known as "cloud access" to software: you reach up and use an application "on a cloud" when you need it; when you don't need it, it stays on the cloud. As e-commerce and business tools on the Internet become widespread, it will lead the entire Internet into a new "Net business" age.

The precondition for all of this to happen is a fertile ecosystem on the Internet that allows for widespread commercial use. In China, such an ecosystem has benefited in recent years from several developments, including government policies and regulations. The Law on Electronic Signatures has been one among many new rules that enhance trustworthiness and safety. Other developments include expanded Internet resources that allow for a wide range of applications on the Internet, and, finally, the sheer number of people using the Internet. The number of users in China broke through 90 million in the year 2004, which represented some 7 percent of China's overall population at the time, and the figure went over 230 million in 2008. The Internet has come to the concerted attention of a large percentage of the Chinese population, who are beginning to use it on a daily basis. Ma feels that the numbers are indicative of a shift in Internet functions inside China that is not only quantitative but also qualitative. The birth of the "Net business" group exposes, at a deeper level, the future direction of e-commerce in China. The growth figures for Alibaba and its C2C sister company Taobao show that businesspeople in China are well aware of the potential of B2B and B2C business, even as the great majority of Internet users are happily wandering in the realm of C2C. "Net business" is growing very quickly, in part spurred on by the proselytizing activities of Jack Ma, but e-commerce is not a simple proposition. Ma emphasizes that it requires an entire infrastructure of support systems, including secure payment, delivery logistics, cooperation with banks, and, of course, government regulations.

To educate policy makers and to bring a critical mass of Internet entrepreneurs together in a kind of lobbying force, Jack Ma created a series of different kinds of conferences. On June 12, 2004, more than a thousand China "Net business" representatives gathered in Hangzhou for the first annual meeting of the Entrepreneurs Summit, also known as the Alifest. The E-Commerce Association and Alibaba hosted the meeting. The gathering of so many senior businesspeople was one indication of the gradual maturing of an interactive Internet business model. Sessions provided an opportunity for Alibaba to display e-commerce methods to China's traditional industries and enterprises. Yahoo!'s co-founder Jerry Yang attended the meeting, expressing surprise at the numbers of people attending. "This is the first time I have even heard people talking about 'Net business,'" he noted. "America doesn't really have this. I myself had not appreciated the usefulness of the Internet as a tool for small and medium-sized enterprises to transact business. Our model is generally just revenue from ads." Ad revenue on the Internet is now around $40 billion, making Jerry Yang's focus on ad revenue understandable.

At the conference, Ma pointed out that the volume of B2B business was a considerable force in China's business world. Four-fifths of China's companies are small and medium-sized enterprises, which in turn produce more than four-fifths of the volume of China's business. Their activities to a large extent influence the entire Chinese economy. Ma went on to say that e-commerce functions on Alibaba are designed with small and medium-sized enterprises in mind. The benefits are apparent: they reduce the number and cost of middleman links, and they prevent small companies from being squeezed and exploited by large ones. Since large buyers purchase in quantity, and since small sellers lack their own sales channels, small companies are generally forced to sell at low prices to the giants. B2B e-commerce Web sites such as Alibaba are now allowing small companies to resolve such problems. In such places as Wenzhou in Zhejiang and Ningpo in Jiangsu, sales transacted on the Internet already constitute a large percentage of total business.

Since 2004, foreign giants have been taking note of this phenomenon, including eBay, Amazon, and other international Internet companies, as well as international investment firms. Wal-Mart attended the conference, as did Ingersoll Rand, Lenovo, and Mitsubishi Heavy Industries. Other traditional industries were there: Japan's Itohchu, Korea's LG Electronics, Korea's Samsung, Sears from the United States, NEC from Japan, and General Motors. A number of these initiated steps to go through Alibaba in purchasing Chinese products. Grassroots-level producers in China were the star of the show, as media began to pay attention to this vital part not just of China's economy but of the global economy. As a result, the conference was also significant at the more profound level of social and cultural exchange.

The vice president of Alibaba, Jin Jianhang, noted, "This gives business back to businessmen. It returns the control of business to those who are actually producing the products."

Hangzhou's Role

How big is the Internet, and how big is e-commerce on the Internet? According to estimates of China's E-Commerce Association, Alibaba, and others, China's e-commerce market will likely exceed $100 billion by the year 2010. Recognizing the groundswell in this business, far more international representatives attended a third Alifest held in Hangzhou in 2006. The opening ceremony on September 9, 2006, was attended by Wal-Mart, Procter & Gamble, Home Depot, and others. They also included Niu Gensheng, chairman of the board of China's Mengniu Group. Niu Gensheng's appearance on the scene was significant, since he is one of the leading businessmen in China. He is now also on the board of the publicly listed company Alibaba.com, which makes it perhaps interesting for the Western investor to know a little about him. Niu is from Inner Mongolia, where he grew up in poverty, but he went on to found the largest milk-products company in China. Legend has it that Niu's father died when he was young, and he was "sold into the city" by relatives in the countryside for a price that is said to have been around $10 at the time (RMB 50). Since the boy did not even know his own surname, he was given the name Niu, "cow," by the father of the family who took him in. This man had started raising cows twenty-eight years earlier when he returned to Inner Mongolia from the Korean War, and so Niu grew up among a herd of cows. When this man died, Niu just kept on raising the cows. Five years later, he was hired by the local milk products factory and was set to work scrubbing bottles. He stayed there sixteen years before starting his own Meng-niu Group (in Chinese, *Meng* means "Mongolia"). The firm later became the largest milk products company in China; now the Mengniu Dairy Company, which is traded on the Hong Kong stock exchange, has a market capitalization of around $6.725 billion.

Two trends had become evident over the years since the first e-commerce conference in 1999. One was the dominance of the city of Hangzhou in China's information industries. Hangzhou is at the forefront of e-commerce and is recognized by many to be the Silicon Valley of China. It lies at the center of the core region of entrepreneurial activity in Zhejiang and is already known as the "capital of Chinese e-commerce." The city's regulatory infrastructure has intentionally incubated a vibrant private economy. In addition, Hangzhou has successfully nurtured human resources with its wealth of scientific and research institutes, IT industries, and Zhejiang University.

A second trend was seen in the depth of the "China shockwave," the degree to which China has become the primary supplier to the world. That wave has owed a certain amount to the use of e-commerce and the ability of China's small companies to access world markets directly.

For both of these reasons, Alibaba considers itself to be a kind of calling card for the city of Hangzhou. Hangzhou in turn serves as a critical home base of government support for Alibaba. According to plan, the information industries in Hangzhou will have increased to 25 percent of Hangzhou's GDP by the year 2010. IT will have become the leading industry in the regional economy, with Alibaba serving as one of its primary contributors.

Alibaba's Goals

Up to now, Alibaba has consistently been able to achieve the goals set by its founder. These were generally regarded with dismay and disbelief, however, when first announced. In 2003, Ma set the goal of an average daily income of $120,000 (RMB 1 million). The previous year, daily income had been only RMB 130,000, so many expressed doubts. Senior managers made a bet against Ma's optimism but were glad, at the end of the year, to have lost. In 2004 Ma set the goal of a daily profit of $120,000 (RMB 1 million) and achieved that as well. In 2005 he set the goal of a daily tax contribution of the same figure and made that. Under Ma's constant pressure and his motivational management, Alibaba's goals have been met.

Ma himself feels that success is dependent on the ability to implement a high degree of efficiency. He regards Alibaba as a team of doers, not a team of thinkers; he says repeatedly that it is better to execute a mistaken decision than it is to muddle around without any decision—what you learn in the course of implementation often gives you the opportunity to move ahead to a higher stage. He agrees with the CEO of Focus Media, Ji-ang Nanchun, who says, "There are plenty of people with bright ideas, but there are very few who can implement bright ideas." Masayoshi Son and Jack Ma have often debated this question: "Is it better to have a third-rate idea and first-rate execution, or is it better to have a first-rate idea and third-rate execution?" and both men have concluded that execution, performance, is key.

What were Ma's goals in 2006? They were less quantified but no less ambitious: to lead the world's "Net people" into the age of "Net business" by executing a global strategy and taking Alibaba into the world. This initial stride out into the world echoed national Chinese policy, which in recent years has been to take China out into the world. It also, however, reinforced Ma's inclinations from the beginning of his business career, due in no small part to his relationship with the Australian couple who served as surrogate parents to Ma and taught him many of the customs of Western culture.

The couple's greatest gift to Ma was to inculcate in him an understanding of Western thinking, which is very different from Chinese thinking, and this was to serve him well in his later career. It was not merely a question of studying language, but rather understanding how Westerners perceive the world and how they interact with people. Social interaction is a key element in business. In the 1980s China was just beginning to emerge from a period of severe isolation. The way people interacted with one another in China during the Communist period, and particularly during the Cultural Revolution, was quite different from the social norms of Americans during the same period. Ma was fortunate to be coached in Western cultural practices while still accessing the local systems of his Chinese life.

Hangzhou was on the periphery of opening up to the West as China began its extraordinary emergence from isolation. This meant that government control over private enterprise in Hangzhou was considerably more lax than it was in urban centers along the coast. In the Zhejiang and Jiangsu regions, state-owned enterprises were not the critical employers that they were, for example, in Shanghai. Zhejiang and Jiangsu were allowed to grow spontaneously, and their rate of growth outstripped that of the rest of China. Jack Ma's exposure to a Western mind-set, through acquaintance with the Australian couple based in Hangzhou, happily coincided with fertile conditions for business.

Unlike many Chinese students who headed overseas to study, Jack Ma was able to absorb the lessons at home. When students who had gone overseas began to return, they found a China that was radically changed. It had moved around them while they were gone, and they had to readapt to new conditions. Jack Ma was already immersed in the new conditions and ahead of his cohort when it came to dealing with the West. Western business had long been yearning to get into the mysterious "Oriental" market and had generally hired the returned Chinese students to help them. In their time abroad, they had undeniably absorbed Western lingo and cultural practices that helped them serve as bridges in cross-cultural business. Nonetheless, they often now lacked a thorough understanding of their homeland. Due to Ma's interaction with a foreign couple, he was equal to any competition, East or West, and this was to be a lifelong benefit to him in business. Because Ma remained at home, rooted in the soil of entrepreneurial southern China and connected to its local leaders, he was able to see opportunities that the returned students missed. When he decided to set up the Alibaba e-commerce Web site in 1999, he saw very clearly that the value chain of this opportunity had two sides to it: overseas buyers and Chinese suppliers. At the time, most business models focused only on the overseas buyers. Returned students focused on these in particular, since that is where their salaries came from. In contrast, Ma focused on the suppliers in China for his revenue.

"At the beginning, I scarcely dared to tell people that we were a Chinese company," Ma says about those days, "because Chinese companies were not highly regarded. Nobody believed that China could produce a good Internet company. That's partly the reason I chose the name Alibaba—it was neither East nor West." At the time, the core IT technology and the subsequent enterprises were all in the West, as were all of the main funding sources. Ma recognized that, even as he remained a Chinese company, he had to use any opportunity to try to get the attention—and support—of foreigners. He recognized that his entire approach needed to be global. If Alibaba were merely Sinocentric, it would be a seller without a buyer. Moreover, Alibaba had to scale up to becoming global very quickly or it would lose its first-to-market advantage in this arena. Ma had no other choice but to make Alibaba a global Web site. As a result, he moved overseas, perhaps too abruptly, but the global impetus was a necessary precondition for later success. He lost a large amount of money, but in the process also built a substantial business base.

In 1999 Jack Ma chose Hong Kong to be the headquarters of the company. Hong Kong's strong international flavor was conducive to expansion abroad, but at the same time Hong Kong was also now part of China, having been returned to China on July 1, 1997. In a ceremony at Hong Kong harbor, the Prince of Wales read a speech on behalf of Queen Elizabeth, boarded the royal yacht, the *Britannia*, and then sailed off into the South China Sea.

Ma had always felt strongly that Alibaba should be thoroughly Chinese, that in the end it would prove to the world that a Chinese company could be a premier multinational in the IT world. In order to attract global human talent, he set up a technology base in America and a branch in London, and then began the arduous process of finding global buyers by making himself into a kind of global sales machine.

The Astronaut

In 1999 and 2000 Ma traveled to some twenty countries, attending business forums, making speeches, and using his silver tongue to promote his B2B thinking and to promote Alibaba. In one month, Ma might go to Europe three times; within a week, he might visit seven countries. He spoke on the BBC, at MIT, at the Wharton School, at Harvard; he spoke at the World Economic Forum, and at the Asian Business Association. Waving his bony hands, he would shout to the audience, "The B2B model will ultimately change the way the globe's millions of businesspeople do business. It will thereby change the lives of billions of people on this earth." The message echoed throughout empty halls at first, but gradually, as the Internet itself changed, the audience for the message increased. "The first time I gave a speech in Germany," Ma recalls, "was when Alibaba already had more than forty thousand members, but in a hall for a thousand people there were exactly three people sitting in the audience. The second time I went to Germany, the hall was full. And some people had flown over from England as well."

Ma's efforts led to an explosive rise in club membership back in China, and revenues of Alibaba quickly rose. Such publications as *Forbes* and *Fortune* took note of Alibaba, and the company began to gain traction as a respectable enterprise. Some of this fame came about despite Ma's speechmaking, because his style has often been self-avowedly "slightly crazy." At Harvard, before giving a speech, he was asked by the host to introduce things about himself that had not been covered in the prepared handout. Stumped for a moment, Ma then responded with an anecdote, "Ten years ago, I applied to come to Harvard. I applied three times and was rejected three times. You all didn't even look at my application, I believe—you just turned me down!" Students were so taken with his candor that thirty-five MBAs lined up after the speech to try to get a job with him.

Other speeches received a less than friendly reception. Chinese companies were beginning to fear the results of entry into the World Trade Organization (WTO), while Western companies were actually becoming afraid of Chinese companies. Ma attended one conference called "China Is a Threat." This seemed ludicrous to those enterprises back home that were saying to themselves, "When we enter the WTO, what are we going to do? Management of overseas firms is better than ours, they have more resources—how can we possibly beat them?" The mutual fear—or, perhaps, lack of understanding—extended to Ma's reception at a BBC interview in London. Ma was asked to prepare for the interview by reading questions on the five subjects that would be covered. He had been told that the interview would be a video-cast, not a direct broadcast, so he did not spend any time review-ing the questions. When the camera started rolling, he heard the host introduce him by saying, "This is BBC headquarters, broad-casting live to the world." The camera turned to him and he was suddenly on the spot, in front of millions of people. Instead of the canned questions, however, he found that the interviewer asked him, in five different ways, whether he really felt he could be suc-cessful as a Chinese company and get rich. Ma later was to com-ment on this experience: "At first, I was shocked into silence. But I kept a smile on my face. My final statement was, 'We will prove that we can survive, and in fact that we can survive pretty well.'"

To do that, Ma recognized that the company had to be inter-national at the same time it developed inside China. The slogan at Alibaba became "Avoid the race inside China; go directly to the global circuit." Ma held on to the dream that one day e-commerce would be a reigning reality, saving costs and allowing global ef-ficiencies in use of resources. At the same time, he believed that Alibaba would become a common asset to the world.

Management

Nobody doubted Jack Ma's ability to talk, but his management decisions leading to the company's wild expansion in 2000 brought Alibaba close to disaster. After the infusions of investment from Goldman Sachs and Softbank—$25 million with which to grow the company—Ma decided to go big. He began to flirt with catastrophe as a result. Alibaba had been established for less than two years and had lost money over the course of that time. In the next brief period, it did worse.

In 2000 Alibaba went to Silicon Valley; it was already set up in Korea, and it rapidly expanded in London and Hong Kong.

Ma soon began to feel that he was losing control. His employees directly under him were world-class professionals, but each felt that his management decisions were correct. The people running Silicon Valley's development center felt that technology was most important to the company. The people running the Hong Kong operation felt that reaching capital markets was most important. Others had opinions as well, and while they fought it out, Ma was silent. To whom should he listen? In which direction should he turn? He didn't know In one year, Alibaba had become a multinational company, with employees from thirteen countries and little idea of how to manage them. "The hardest thing in the world is to have fifty hypersmart people sitting together in one room, trying to get something done," as he later summed up the situation.

To compound the problems, Ma had based Alibaba's English-language Web site in Silicon Valley. Only after this move did he discover that Silicon Valley's employees were all "techies," whereas what the Web site really needed was people who understood business. All of the people who knew business, however, were based in New York. They now had to be transferred to Silicon Valley, and those costs were extremely high. "It was an incredibly stupid thing to do," recalls Ma. "Imagine trying to get everyone around the globe to come to Silicon Valley to work." At the same time, Nasdaq was plunging and investors were running scared: as the Chinese saying goes, every bush and tree looked like an enemy. Extreme nervousness pervaded the market; a large number of Internet companies closed down, and Alibaba's Silicon Valley office rode uncomfortably in the middle of all the stormy weather.

Ma realized that without taking definitive action, the company was going to go under. He announced a reduction in forces at the end of 2000, a strategic contraction that he now calls "returning to China." This action brought about low morale. Pessimism swept the company, and only Ma's extraordinary ability to motivate people with his ideas prevented key talented people from leaving. The most urgent thing facing the company after this return to China was an overall improvement in the quality of the enterprise. An experienced manager by the name of Guan Mingsheng was brought in to do this. Guan became COO in January 2001, after sixteen years of experience at General Electric. With Guan's assistance, Jack Ma was able to turn the company around.

At the same time, Ma narrowed the focus of the company to its original goals and purposes. He told employees, "If you want to work at Alibaba, your daily work has to focus on our three main goals. If you feel we are crazy in doing this, then please leave. If you are just waiting for us to take the company public, then please leave. If you are bringing individual perspectives to the company that are not beneficial to our overall goals, please leave. And if you are restless and dissatisfied, please leave." The attitude of many employees improved after this direct approach.

SARS

Severe acute respiratory syndrome (SARS) is a highly contagious form of pneumonia. In the spring of 2003, this disease became a scare that swept throughout China. Few who lived through those days can forget them. Government offices and businesses shut down. If you had to go outside, you wore a mask. Cities were suddenly ghostly in their silence. People were afraid: nobody knew how bad the epidemic might become. Nurses and others in health-related professions were at risk; Beijing, Guangzhou, and other places were eventually quarantined, but not before an Alibaba employee had contracted the virus at the Canton trade fair.

The Canton Fair is held twice a year, once in the spring and once in the fall. It is a highly lucrative trade event, and government authorities were reluctant to shut down the fair when uncertain news of an uncertain virus began to circulate. The spring fair in 2003 opened as usual, and an Alibaba employee who attended on behalf of the company became infected. A financial reporter named Zheng Zuoshi, who was conducting interviews at Alibaba at the time, wrote:

> Alibaba's "China Supplier Programs" include a promise to help customers at all kinds of trade fairs. Naturally, this includes the country's largest trade fair, at Canton. Canton (Guangzhou in Chinese) had clearly been recognized as an infected area by the time of the opening ceremony of the fair, but the national government did not take action and quarantine the event. As a result, Alibaba felt it was obliged to carry through on its promise and accompany customers to the fair. The Alibaba employee who was responsible for this duly went to the fair and did her job, but soon after returning to Hangzhou she began to feel sick. She began to show signs of infection. Nevertheless, as a diligent employee, she came to work and therefore had contact with many other employees. It was unknown how many people she might have infected.
>
> When it was finally realized that the employee had contracted SARS, Alibaba quickly became the focal point of tremendous concern. The entire working area of the company was sealed off, and essentially all employees were quarantined at home. A small group of employees had been secretly working offsite on the Taobao Web site, so they were outside the danger zone. The mayor of Hangzhou had visited Alibaba, however, so [he] was quarantined, as well as his entire entourage.

Later, when all were off quarantine, Ma would walk along the streets of Hangzhou and people would point at him and say, "Look, there goes the SARS man."

SARS arrived just at a time when development work at Alibaba was proceeding at a feverish pace, as the company faced deadlines for the Taobao and Alibaba Web sites. Quarantined employees were able to work at home, but this in itself was a new experience, and they lacked logistical support and hands-on management. Senior managers began arranging for broadband Internet connections, establishing communications links, and reorganizing the technical department in order to network computers. The atmosphere was one of extreme crisis: nobody had full confidence in what might lie ahead. Then there were questions from families of employees: "Why did you allow an Alibaba employee to go into the heart of the SARS epidemic? What's wrong with you? To think only of business at a time like this!" Ma felt the criticism like proverbial spears pointing at his body. Faced with tremendous pressure, he had to respond. He felt somewhat responsible and yet not totally so, since the Chinese government had refused to close down the fair. Still, he felt he had to give comfort to his staff. The night before the quarantine began, he sat down to compose a letter to his employees and their relatives. A condensed version follows.

Dear Ali friends and relatives,

My heart is heavy. I extend my profound apologies to you all. Since learning the results of the test [of our colleague], I can tell you that if there were anything I could do to transform our sick colleague into a healthy one, I would do it. I am putting everything I have into guaranteeing the health of everyone.

Explanations are meaningless today. The thing has already happened. I regret not taking all preventive measures in time. Our preparatory measures were perhaps the best in all of Hangzhou, but due to unforeseen factors, we were hit by SARS.

It is true that inadequacies exist in Alibaba, and there are many questions we will address after the crisis. I take all responsibility, as the person in charge. But reason tells me that now is not the time for recriminations and complaints. Right now, we have to join hands in meeting the challenges ahead. Our young company, made up of young people, will be maturing much faster, I believe, as a result of this crisis.

I have been moved in these past few days by the sight of all Ali people choosing an attitude of optimism and fortitude. We are concerned about each other and we support each other. Sooner or later, this crisis will end and life will continue: the calamity will not stop us from continuing on our mission. I am very proud of our young people because of this. I am proud to be working in this kind of company. I hope that family and friends of Ali people will applaud young people like these, who dare to face challenges. They did not panic nor did they retreat. This is a function of our sense of values, which I believe all Ali people truly understand.

From tonight, all Alibaba employees in Hangzhou will be completely quarantined. On behalf of the safety of ourselves, our families and friends, and also on behalf of the future of Alibaba, we will all be passing the next few days locked up. I understand everyone's feelings and I am truly sorry to have to influence the lives of everyone in this way. Taking care of our health is more important than anything. I ask everyone to conform in a most conscientious manner to the rules. Please share this letter with your respected relatives and friends. Please express my profound apologies to them as well.

Let us wish our colleague a speedy recovery. I will be in touch with everyone via the Internet in the next days. As always, we will be objective and transparent with any further information as the situation develops.

Good health to all,

Ali-person
Jack Ma

Later public management studies showed that the one critical aspect that was lacking and that turned the SARS episode into a far worse crisis than it might have been was prompt and open communication. The crisis was a "sudden mass event," and handling of such things is now known to require timely communication. This letter from Jack Ma not only helped calm things down in the company but also pacified the emotions of relatives and helped win public support.

Alibaba employees were quarantined for about eight or nine days, during which time they continued to work via computer and telephone. In the end, nobody other than the initial employee contracted SARS, and she quickly regained her health. In Beijing and other major cities, the disruption was more severe: many offices closed for weeks, and the toll on the country's economy as well as its reputation was heavy. Alibaba came through the experience unscathed and with a sense of cohesiveness and esprit de corps that had been missing previously. Despite the SARS interruption, Alibaba increased its revenue by over five times in 2003, and accomplished what to some was seen as a miracle of bringing average daily income to more than RMB 1 million.

Maoist Management Practices

Prior to the SARS crisis, Ma had not only led the company through the "severe winter" of the dot-com bust but also through the consequences of his own inexperience in managing a rapidly growing company. To turn the company around, he now instituted stringent belt-tightening policies. These had a definite Maoist flavor to them.

The Internet had reached the bottom of its trough at the end of the year 2000, and as head of Alibaba, Jack Ma brought his team home to China. People began to have skeptical feelings about the Internet during this period, but Ma's confidence was unshaken. Unlike most, he was lucky to have enough funding to carry on the work of creating a solid company of considerable depth. "Our slogan, in the midst of this wintertime in the business, is 'just hanging on to life is a victory in itself.' We believe that the Internet will fire up again. All we have to do is survive. Not dying gives us hope." In order to rouse employees to a similar optimism, Ma began to use old Communist Chinese phrases about the spirit of the Long March, the strategic retreat of the Red Army during 1934–36 that led to the rise of Mao Zedong. Ma likened his staff to troops of the Red Army, and the vocabulary of the corporation's campaigns became imbued with revolutionary fervor. This was in line with management practices in other Chinese corporations, which have absorbed the disciplining and inspirational methods of earlier Maoist days. Alibaba's campaigns took their guiding messages from recent history and the tenacity of the guerrilla fighters during the Anti-Japanese War (1937–1945) and the Chinese Civil War (which ended in 1949). Alibaba first had the "Yan'an Rectification Movement," harking back to the guerrilla base in Shaanxi Province in northwest China, where Mao Zedong and others had holed up at the end of the Long March. This was designed to root out opposition to Mao's leadership and thus align all energies in a unified direction. Back in 1942, more than 10,000 people were killed in the process, so the concept of "rectification" in China carries with it a fearsome sense of culling the ranks.

Next came the "Military and Politics University of the Anti-Japanese Invasion." Once an institute dedicated to the training of military translators, again during the Yan'an period in Chinese Communist history, it involved regimented intense training during a national crisis, appropriate for Alibaba after the Internet bubble burst and so many companies were failing. Finally came

"Opening Up the Wastelands," echoing the pioneering spirit that sent people to the western Chinese territories to begin the Sinification of those lands.

From 2001 to 2003, the period in which Alibaba faced its most urgent crises, Ma promoted these Maoist management campaigns because he felt that they were effective ways to reform the company in this particular period. The first campaign, Yan'an Rectification, was intended to unify views and strengthen confidence; the second, Military and Politics University, was intended to cultivate a professional cadre of team managers. "Through these campaigns, we purged ourselves of people who did not share common goals and a sense of mission," Ma stated, but he was seen by many as harsh and heavy-handed.

Alibaba had been functioning as a kind of guerrilla operation, Ma told his company, and now it was time to create a "proper army that could fight tough battles." At the same time, he intentionally kept a degree of flexibility in the company, aware of the dangers of rigid authoritarianism. Somebody once asked him if it was more important to make money first, or to train people first. He responded with what he called his "yes theory": "Yes, it is important to make money and to train." Do you want obedient employees or capable employees? "Yes. You need both obedience and capability." Do you go for the dream or for the reality? "Yes. You go for both." System or people: which is more important? "Yes: both are important. We move forward together." His point in making this kind of argument was that Alibaba needed a diversity of viewpoints and talents. Ma did not want to direct everyone's thinking down the same channel.

The third and final campaign was aimed at training salespeople in the concepts and attitudes they should use toward customers. This involved methods and concrete skills. "The most important thing is to help the customer make money. Most enterprises are thinking of how they can take the five dollars in a customer's pocket out of there and put it into their own pocket. What we want to do is help that customer turn his five dollars into fifty dollars, and then from that fifty take our five." Ma spent a large amount of money on this concept and on the Web functions to implement it. He believes his adherence to this concept is the reason the company is successful today.

In terms of his management style, many have regarded Ma as a kind of madman—too punctilious about details and too reliant on a long-term vision. Ma has always shrugged off the criticism. "I long ago stopped being concerned about how people regarded me. If I cared, Alibaba would not have survived to today. We have been so abused by others that our skin is tough as leather. Knives can't get through, bullets either." In the end, Ma and senior management wrote up a constitution for the company that was intended to "enable Alibaba to continue to grow for 102 years," and incorporated the highest principles of the company. Its first item: "Everything changes. The only thing that does not change is change itself." By understanding this fundamental principle, one could mentally prepare for change and be able to make use of it. The second item: "Always make a reasonable and fair profit. Making outrageous amounts of money is not your first priority."

After going through these three campaigns and the exercise of drawing up principles, Ma was surprised to discover that the company was showing signs of real change. Employees were maturing, customers increasing, and new members piling in. The company was both growing fast and developing a stable foundation. Alibaba was changing from a pheasant into a phoenix. From being a guerrilla band of farmers with rifles, it had turned into a regular army. Ma himself was becoming more comfortable at managing a business that was inventing new models as it moved into an unknown, changing world. Most importantly, the business model of Alibaba was becoming clearer. Investors were increasingly confident about it, as were employees, and this helped propel the company in a unified direction. The model was based on making money from fees from China Suppliers rather than from a percentage of each Internet transaction or from advertising revenue. To draw in China Suppliers who were willing to cough up membership fees, Alibaba had to create a tremendous platform, stock it with large quantities of information, and thereby attract the eyes of buyers and sellers. Overseas promotion drew in buyers, while the small and medium-sized enterprises within China provided the revenue.

This model was increasingly effective as information flow increased. The volume of information flowing daily through Alibaba was between five and eight times that of its closest competitor. By providing a real service to Chinese companies and thus serving a real need, Alibaba began to stand out ahead of the rest of the Internet pack. In a moment of braggadocio, Ma is quoted as saying, "You couldn't see the rest of the competition with a telescope."

Zhejiang Province is famous in China for having a high concentration of successful businesspeople. These people are known especially for their frugality, their quick response in snapping up opportunities, and their tenacity in sheer survival. In the IT world, other successful Zhejiang entrepreneurs include Ding Lei, Qian Zhonghua, and Chen Tianqiao, whose wealth is measured in the billions of U.S. dollars. Like these men, Ma knows how to make money by properly husbanding it. One prime example: there is a piggy bank on the photocopy machine inside the door of the Alibaba offices. On the wall above it is a list of rules about using the machine. Anything over 150 copies has to be registered at the front desk, since the common practice in China is to copy your child's textbooks at the company machine. Costs are carefully controlled at Alibaba. Coming through that same door has been an endless stream of potential investors, and the two are closely related.

Internet companies that survived the bursting of the dot-com bubble and that were good at allocating carefully tended resources were companies that invited more attention. In 2004, such companies became the target of a kind of investing frenzy. The 2004 phenomenon, as it is called, relates to the increase in money looking for good investments in China. In 2004, however, Jack Ma was not in favor of adding to his investor commitments. He had analyzed Alibaba's needs and decided that "we don't want to list [on the stock market] just in order to list. Listing should be a means to really growing the company, not just to getting some fast money." He noted the headaches of the three large portals in China, and the fact that they could think only of the next season, how to make the numbers in the next quarter. "Our funding right now allows us to think three years down the road in how to position ourselves. If you don't go public, you have five investors sitting in front of you with whom you have to deal. If you go public, you have five thousand. I'm not afraid of it; the time just hasn't yet arrived."

Swordplay on the West Lake

One of the primary reality checks for Jack Ma in evaluating the direction of the IT industry and his own needs for funding has been a series of annual conferences called the Swordplay Conferences, initiated by Ma and held on the shores of West Lake in Hangzhou. The first conference convened on September 10, 2000, and since then the event has become a summit for China's leaders in both Internet and overall economic spheres. The conferences use a unique format that has become a showcase for China's emerging new-economy industries. In 2000, the five big bosses of the Internet in China gathered to test their "swordplay" in discussing

Internet issues. These five included Sohu's CEO, Zhang Chaoyang; Sina's president, Wang Zhidong; NetEase's chairman of the board, Ding Lei; the chairman of the board of 8848 (the company named for the height of Mt. Everest in meters), Wang Juntao; and Alibaba's CEO, Jack Ma. A renowned author of martial arts novels, Jin Yong, was persuaded to be master of ceremonies.

Jin Yong has played an important role in Jack Ma's life and in his business philosophy. Relatively unknown in the West, his is a household name in China. Jin Yong is the pen name; his real name is Louis Cha. The Cha family has been one of the great names in southern China, well known for commercial success but also for a sense of civic responsibility. The family originally hailed from Zhejiang province, but many members dispersed after the Communist takeover of China, and one branch continued in Hong Kong. That branch has included major figures in real estate, finance, and philanthropy, and it has also included the spectacularly successful author Louis Cha. Born in Zhejiang in 1924, Cha has lived most of his life in Hong Kong. Dozens of his novels have become the inspiration not only for movies and martial arts advocates but also for many of China's senior businessmen. The novels incorporate Chinese history and philosophy. Their lessons, imbued with the spirit of "rivers and lakes," that mystical realm of right-thinking brotherhood among outlaws, are often cited by Jack Ma in his management practices.

The title of the Hangzhou conferences paid homage to this *wu xia* or martial arts tradition. When Ma first began these conferences, he knew he had to attract the leaders in the Chinese IT field, and he knew that the best way to do this was to draw them by using a famous personality as host. Nobody inside the IT industry would do: they were not disinterested and they lacked the moral stature. Jack Ma had never met Louis Cha, but he had read all of his books.

Jack Ma worshiped Cha, and since his early childhood, he

had been a martial arts fanatic. Too, very few people in China do not know the pen name Jin Yong. His novels have sold more than one hundred million copies in China; senior businesspeople, including Ding Lei and others, are simply addicted to them. In 2000, CCTV shot a forty-part series that was adapted from one of Cha's novels. Ma determined that he had to meet the man, and he proceeded to find a way to be introduced. When the two finally met for a meal in Hong Kong, Cha calligraphed a couplet for him, which Ma has hanging behind his desk at his office to this day: *Rather than stand idly by the pond, longing for fish, far better to go out and make a net.*

In 2000 Louis Cha came to speak at the Zhejiang University Business Training Center, and Ma was able to have long talks with him about such things as martial arts moves (*wu gong*), schools of thought in *weiqi* (or Go, a board game that requires great strategic thinking), *taijiquan*, and swordplay. Most of the talking was done by Ma, however. Louis Cha reportedly sat there smiling and nodding. Later, Ma was chagrined and embarrassed enough to say, "You would have thought I had written all those novels myself!" Nonetheless, the two men hit it off, and Cha agreed to come to Hangzhou to talk about *weiqi*, drink a little Shaoxing wine, and continue their discussion. Both men loved the board game; both felt that "people are like *weiqi* pieces, and the world is like a huge *weiqi* board." After this visit in Hangzhou, Ma felt comfortable enough to ask Louis Cha to serve as master of ceremonies at the Hangzhou conference. Even though a few of Ma's colleagues had advised him against even trying, Ma simply called him on the phone and posed the question, and Cha agreed.

Many elements of Louis Cha's novels can be used to symbolize the catalyzing thrust of the Internet in today's world. Ma feels strongly that the "realm of rivers and lakes" can be usefully compared to the Internet itself, and that techniques used by the brotherhood of outlaws can be adapted for modern-day business. For example, Ma believes that Internet enterprises have to develop a thick outer skin in order to grow and develop—they have to disregard criticism and hold fast to their own mission. At the same time, they have to practice *qigong,* or internal breathing techniques, particularly when cultivating management talent. He feels that all Internet companies have similar "internal breath" issues, issues that must be handled with great care. These include attracting top talent, keeping good employees, cultivating managers, and building a culture with common core values.

At the 2000 Swordplay conference, Ma addressed the question of what he felt the Internet would be like in five years. "Many people ask me what things will be like. I think that five years from now, no one will be talking about the Internet. Twenty years ago color television was the rage, but nobody even talks about color televisions today. They have been absorbed into daily life. The Internet will be the same. It will be so embedded in people's lives that talking about it will be way behind the times."

Second Swordplay Conference: Alibaba's Changing Battle Array

The soft light over the West Lake in Hangzhou on October 21, 2001, intoxicated all those strolling along its waters. They included some senior players. After a turbulent year, Internet "masters" were again meeting to test their swords at the second conference. Most of the previous attendees were there, plus two new ones. Louis Cha again attended, and Jack Ma again took center stage. In his opening speech, Ma emphasized the most significant quality of the Internet: change. He noted that the quality of that change itself had shifted, however, and that guerrilla tactics were now less helpful in meeting challenges; instead, he personally was building a standard army that could, as he said, "line up in a proper battle array." In earlier years, one had to remain nimble and change fast. For the past two years, he felt it had been best to stay quiet, practicing *qigong* techniques. He said that what Alibaba needed now was to forget about practicing "moves," again a reference to martial arts training. Instead, it needed to focus on building a unified team. The age of the lone ranger in the Internet was gone. The age of team spirit and coordinated action had arrived.

When Alibaba was first established, Ma conceded, they had felt like ancient warrior heroes. "I was proud of that. Now it is time to turn those heroes into a proper army. We still need three more years before we can start making real money, and it won't happen without properly trained forces. Then, by the time I'm forty, I want to retire and go back to teaching in school. I plan to teach everyone about Alibaba's thousand and one mistakes!"

Third Swordplay Conference: Giving Business Back to Businesspeople

The third Swordplay Conference was held on November 3, 2002. Some of the old Internet masters were quietly gone, while others had taken their place. Attending were Tengxun's CEO, Ma Huateng; the president of 3721, Zhou Hongwei (the name comes from $3 \times 7 = 21$, which in Chinese means something akin to "just do it"); the CEO of Youcheng, Liang Jianzhang; and the president of Lianzhong, Bao Qiuqiao. The host was the CCTV personality Zhang Wei. This new aristocracy of the Internet was, in one way or another, in the process of using the Internet to change people's daily lives. The generally loquacious Jack Ma stayed on the sidelines that year, listening. It had become apparent to all that a major restructuring of human communications was under way and that the ramifications were enormous. Many were not able to sit back and think through the consequences, to consider how the moving pieces on the *weiqi* board of our planet would be shifting like tectonic plates.

The recovery of the Internet economy gave the sessions an unprecedented sense of confidence. Gone were the questions of whether it was better to burn money or to make money, to make a profit or not. Instead, the sessions discussed what benefits the Internet would bring to society at large, and in particular the benefits to China's economy. How should Internet companies plan for their own future after starting to make money? The overall topic of the meeting was therefore "After the bubble: The Internet Changing People's Lives." Jack Ma summarized three main differences of this conference from the previous ones. First of all, the primary topic was different. Second, the participants were different: the portals had dominated the first conference, while lifestyle services companies had dominated the second. The third difference was that Alibaba, initiator and organizing unit of the conferences, was not attending in force this year since it was putting all its energies into setting up a new platform. Though quieter this time around, Ma was just as wiry and energetic as ever. His message was that the "crouching tiger, hidden dragon" of China's Internet was still capable of delivering shocks to the industry every day. The 2003 conference recognized that more people must be allowed to appreciate the Internet's benefits, particularly more small businesspeople.

In April 2003, Jack Ma registered the name of the conferences as a company-owned trademark. "West Lake Swordplay Conference" was becoming a generally used term in China, even a kind of synonym for the Internet itself. The conferences were also helping define how China would participate in an Internet-linked world, how the country felt about the sociopolitical impact of this empowering technology.

Fourth Swordplay Conference:
Walking on Two Legs

The fourth West Lake Swordplay Conference began behind closed doors on the banks of West Lake on November 3, 2003. Attending were Softbank president Masayoshi Son, Tom.com Internet Group president Wang Leilei, Tengxun CEO Ma Huateng, Shanda Internet CEO Chen Tianqiao, Youcheng CEO Liang Jianzhang, Baidu president Li Yanhong, and Alibaba CEO Jack Ma. The topic for this year's conference was "China: The Next Wave." But could anyone really know what the future might hold?

This year was the first time the conference had closed its sessions to the media, which piqued the curiosity of all, especially the press. Supposedly it was top-secret and yet everyone knew all about the fact that it was being held. Ma explained that many of the companies attending were in the midst of preparations to list on the stock exchange, and so it would be inconvenient for them to reveal much to the press. One thing that nobody could avoid noticing, despite the secrecy, was the attendance of Softbank's Masayoshi Son. This brought together two crucial but very different groups at the conference: Internet companies and venture capital firms.

As mentioned earlier, Masayoshi Son had become one of the richest men in Asia during the boom years in Japan. In 1981 he returned to Japan from Berkeley to start a company called Softbank Capital, with initial capital coming primarily from loans from banks. In 1995 he was successful in buying Ziff-Davis Media for $2.1 billion, after an earlier unsuccessful attempt. In 1995 he spent $100 million on 37 percent of Yahoo! at a time when it had only seventeen employees. Son then went on to make other investments and acquisitions, turning Softbank into a primary investor in new technology. At its peak, Softbank was valued at around $140 billion, of which Son owned more than half. He sold some of the Yahoo! shares in order to finance other acquisitions, moving from 37 percent down to 7 percent. As of October 2006, the name by which Softbank is now known is Softbank Telecom Corp., of which Masayoshi Son is chairman and CEO.

Alibaba had always been in the public eye during the Swordplay conferences, particularly as the originator of the event. During 2003, the company had been particularly pressworthy because of its investment in the wholly new endeavor called Taobao. The name implies "searching for treasure," which echoes the treasure theme of Alibaba and also makes the Internet seem a good place to prospect.

Taobao was set up to be a C2C business, for consumer-to-consumer transactions. This was quite different from Alibaba's formerly steadfast emphasis on being a service company for enterprises. The standard line had been that Alibaba intended to increase the wealth of its enterprise partners, whereby it would increase its own profit. Taobao, on the other hand, was clearly for individual consumers. There was a plausible rationale, because Taobao aimed to make everyone a businessperson, a buyer or seller who could engage in transactions via the Internet. From being a service provider for enterprises to creating a transaction platform for individuals was a shift, however. Alibaba threw out an additional bombshell in summer 2003 when it declared it was investing $12 million (RMB 100 million) in the project, which later rose to $55 million (RMB 450 million). The B2B giant had now also become a C2C giant. Jack Ma was clearly moving in the direction of what the Chinese call "walking on two legs," or relying on two different income streams. This was hedging his bets *and* making sure he occupied the space with the most potential for growth. Ma fully intended to ensure the success of his long-term objective of creating a company that would last for 102 years.

Fifth Swordplay Conference:
Cloud-Style *Taijiquan*

Jack Ma's Chinese name is Ma Yun, which means "horse clouds." In martial arts, cloud-style *taijiquan* is a form of movement that simulates the softness yet invisible power of clouds. Cyclical movements with the hands turn back on themselves as the clouds (or fists— *quan* in Chinese) reach an extreme, or *taiji*, and then fold back toward the center. All is contained within the cycle, and the physical or mental movement connecting extremes is a matter of balance. As a practitioner of *taijiquan*, Ma was glad to describe this movement one morning on November 4, 2004, to President Bill Clinton, who was attending a Swordplay Conference and also meeting with the six giants of China's Internet world. They included Yahoo!'s cofounder Yang Zhiyuan (Jerry Yang); Alibaba's CEO, Jack Ma; Ding Lei, chairman of the board of NetEase; the president and CEO of Tengxun, Ma Huateng; Sohu's chairman of the board and CEO, Zhang Chaoyang; and Sina's CEO and president, Wang Yan. Together with Clinton, the seven were dubbed the "Seven Samurai" by outsiders, after the characters in the well-known Akira Kurosawa film. Furthermore, the famous economist Zhang Weiying, vice president of the Guanghua School of Management at Peking University, served as host for this session of the Hangzhou West Lake Swordplay Conference. The future of China's Internet was discussed in depth. Jerry Yang's participation in this meeting titillated those who wanted to figure out how Yahoo! and Alibaba might combine forces. Ma remained coy on that subject, choosing instead to talk about competition. Ding Lei had not taken the whole arena of e-commerce seriously, which was lucky for Alibaba. "Sometimes not being taken seriously is a stroke of good luck, for other people aren't trying to kill you to get into your business. If [Ding Lei] had been more attentive, none of the good stuff would have been left over for me," stated Ma.

Ma spoke at length about one of his favorite subjects, *taijiquan*. "I practice *taijiquan*, which requires focus," he told Clinton. "Don't think it's just waving your hands around this way and that. In fact, you have to keep your entire self fixed on one spot, one focus. You use your balance and the right sense of timing to know when to attack. So in Jin Yong's novels, I particularly appreciate it when the Yellow Master appears. Nobody pays much attention to this old man. Nobody is on guard against him, till he suddenly makes a move and tosses the person that everyone thinks is most capable into the river. It is very important to choose the right moment to make your move."

Known for his loquaciousness, Ma appeared quite comfortable comparing himself to the master of Jin Yong's novels. It is true that cloud-style *taijiquan* can serve as powerful mental training; it was also true that Ma was clearly considering when to make his move. This was not lost on anyone at the conference. Less than one year later, Alibaba would announce its marriage to Yahoo! which would bring in a dowry in the neighborhood of $1 billion.

Alibaba's Use of Human Resources

"If you can win people's hearts, you can rule all under heaven," and "Human talent is the greatest asset; success or failure depends on people," are truisms that show up in a myriad of ways in Chinese philosophy and also in the most ancient classics. Various sages sum up how to manage chaos using the same concept of effective management of people. For example, *Journey to the West* is a Chinese classic that has been mined for its pearls of wisdom and which Ma feels is relevant in this context. The book is about the journey of a Buddhist priest to India, accompanied by his loyal companions, including a monkey and a pig. Many people read *Journey to the West* for entertainment; Jack Ma reads it for its guidance in business.

Stories from this classic date from hundreds of years earlier but were stitched together into a novel in the 1590s, during the late Ming dynasty. A man named Wu Cheng'en is credited with authorship. Ma identifies not with Monkey, who is fantastic in his supernatural powers, but rather with the more prosaic leader, the Buddhist priest Tang Seng [Priest Tang]. Monkey, whose name is Sun Wukong, or "Sun who Comprehends the Great Void," is enlightened but also unruly and uncontrollable. He is master of technology and magical powers. Ma regards himself as someone who is ignorant of technology, while Alibaba is positioned as a technology-based Internet company. As Tang Seng needed Monkey for his skills on the journey westward, so Alibaba needs a core group of people who are attuned to computers and mathematics. Instead of using technical language to guide these people, though, Ma uses old-fashioned inspiration. He uses intuition and emotionally based language and culture to manage and lead a group of people whom he recognizes are hyperrational and cognitively inclined.

"Intelligent people need a fool to lead them," Ma says about his application of the principles of *Journey to the West*. "When the team's all a bunch of scientists, it is best to have a peasant lead the way. His way of thinking is different. It's easier to win if you have people seeing things from different perspectives."

Ma has borrowed extensively from *Journey to the West* in his concept of teamwork among disparate kinds of people. He calls this idea "Priest Tang" teamwork. "Priest Tang did not have such great native abilities; everyone knows that. But he had phenomenal willpower. He was unwilling to give up until he had gotten hold of the true sutras, or precepts. On the other hand, Monkey, Sun Wukong, had abilities that were extraordinary. You couldn't do without him, but you absolutely did not want too many of him in your company."

Ma feels that the question of whether Alibaba can realize its mission depends entirely on the overall abilities of its team. The social technology of this team is paramount, the way it is organized to work smoothly together. To create this winning team, he does not want too many heroes—heroes are capable of turning on one another. He also does not want too much excellence, since you need common people to get things done. Ma's "Priest Tang–style team" works well: Tang was a fine leader because he kept his eye on the goal; Monkey (Sun Wukong) was the backbone of the enterprise because of his talents, but he also brought grief to the leaders with his foibles; the pig, Zhu Ba Jie, was limited in his abilities but he was loyal and protected his master at critical times. All of these types were necessary for success.

At the same time, all team members have to adhere to the same values in order to accomplish a common mission. The first rule Ma has tried to inculcate at Alibaba is to be happy in what one is doing. Only if employees are happy can customers be happy. Only if customers are happy can the enterprise be profitable. This is another way of saying "customers first." There are benefits of putting the message in this circuitous fashion because it brings a group of superior talent under firm command. Alibaba's salaries have always been low compared to those in the general marketplace. Many employees and managers come into the company with a base salary of less than half of what they had been earning elsewhere. Ma has not hidden the fact that in the early days this was different and a considerable amount of money was spent on senior management outside of China. "We discovered they did not come up to expectations," Ma has explained tersely, "and so these people were the first to be fired."

As someone who has clear ideas of what he wants and what he does not want, Ma has made every effort to put these ideas into companywide practice. He has reinforced the understanding that "Jack Ma will only fight together with people who have the same set of values as he does." In order to clarify values, he has come up with slogans and sayings that keep people on target. "Internet companies survive only if everyone has the same purpose," he has said. "In the Internet, you can't have people working in their separate departments on disparate things. Everything has to be unified and for the same purpose. Internet companies have to harmonize, which means teamwork and common energies." The dynamic nature of teamwork is key. This oft-stated emphasis is in part because departments in traditional industries in China have been allowed to work as separate fiefdoms. Indeed, the entire governmental structure of pre-market-economy China reinforced the de facto practice of competing loyalties and hidden agendas. Ma battles that with his ideas of teamwork, and he is successful in part because of the youth of the people he has attracted.

Using a "Happy Culture" to Attract Talent

Alibaba is considered to be a stingy company. It has assets in the hundreds of millions but puts very little money into advertising or publicity, and its employee salaries are low. One reason is that its funding initially came from venture capital and had to be conserved. Another is that Alibaba is not interested in attracting people on the basis of high promises; it wants to attract them on the basis of its corporate culture. Alibaba "never voluntarily takes actions that poach people from other companies," but at the same time, many people have been attracted to Alibaba precisely because of its spirit.

A key part of the corporate culture that Ma tries to emphasize is a flattening of hierarchy, a lessening of the distance between levels of command. "There is no distance between Jack Ma and the rest of us," a young employee explained. "This surprises people, but in fact it's true." Another stated, "Alibaba is a company that doesn't wear clothes. It doesn't have layer upon layer of coats like other companies—you pull off one layer and there's another. With us, what you see is what we are."

CCTV holds a contest called Best Employer of the Year every year, and Alibaba was selected one of China's Ten Best in 2005. Ma was pleased, since he had followed a policy of "happy work" corporate culture for years and felt that he was now reaping the rewards. "Employees can wear sandals to work at Alibaba," he noted in his acceptance speech for this prize, "and they can come into my office anytime. In brief, we want employees to be joyful."

A number of the senior management team at Alibaba have been with Ma for the whole length of Alibaba's history. Li Qi is the current COO, Sun Danyu is general manager of Taobao, and Jin Jianhang is deputy vice president of Alibaba. They were among the original eighteen that founded the company. "Like me," Ma has said, "they are not necessarily the most absolutely intelligent people, but we have all matured over these years."

Using Charisma to Attract Talent

Charisma involves a kind of magnetic appeal, the indefinable ability of a leader to get people to do things for him. It takes charisma to make warriors charge into the breach, and also to get highly intelligent people to bow their backs to hard work for a common cause. Cai Chongxin's entry into the company was undoubtedly evidence that there was something about Jack Ma that one could call charisma.

Originally from Taiwan, Cai has a law degree from Yale and, before he joined Alibaba, was serving as Asian representative of the venture capital firm Invest AB. Prior to the 2007 reorganization, he served as head of finances of the overall company; the CFO of the listed company Alibaba.com is now Maggie Wu.

"Cai Chongxin is in charge of talking to investors," explained Ma as preparations began for listing Alibaba.com on the Hong Kong market. "When I have an idea that might have any kind of impact on shareholder interests, I first talk it through with Cai Chongxin. When he understand it, he is the one who then goes back to talk to investors until they understand it too." Cai's role is critical in the eyes of Jack Ma and Alibaba. He joined the company in April 1999, taking a mere $60 (500 RMB) in monthly salary. He had met Jack Ma when discussing investment from a company called Invest AB. After talking to him for a while, Cai unexpectedly said, "Jack Ma, I want to sit on your side. I want to join Alibaba!" Ma was dubious about how this would work, but Cai persuaded him and also persuaded his wife. She later noted that her husband would never have forgiven her if she had not agreed to his joining Alibaba. Cai came in as CFO.

Mission, Values, Trustworthiness

In 2001 Jack Ma had a fortuitous breakfast meeting with Bill and Hillary Clinton. He came away from this meeting with a strong sense of the importance of mission, both to a country, as described by the Clintons, and to a corporation. Bill Clinton had told him that in leading a country forward and knowing in which direction it should go, the critical thing was a sense of mission. A leader had to use the country's own sense of mission as its motivating force. This was helpful to Ma, since at the time he knew that Internet companies in China were groping forward painfully, trying to copy Yahoo! as well as America Online and Amazon. They were trying to emulate someone else. This reinforced his belief that Alibaba needed to have its own direction. "We can only follow our own sense of mission" became his mantra after that breakfast meeting.

He later commented on that breakfast and the importance of mission repeatedly in speeches that he made in China. "Some time ago," he would say, "I attended the World Economic Forum and I heard CEOs from the Fortune 500 talking mostly about 'mission' and 'sense of values.' Chinese enterprises rarely talk about these things. If you do, people think you are full of hot air and stop talking to you. But our enterprises lack these, and I believe that it will prevent them from developing into major companies as a consequence."

By the year 2000, Ma and his team had determined that the mission of Alibaba was to "make it easy to do business anywhere." All of the services, systems, and software of the company were being created in order for Alibaba to make business easy for customers. Under this guiding mission, Alibaba began to form its own set of values, which it institutionalized into a list of nine items, then later condensed to six. The process of delineating these values began in 2001. At the time, Alibaba employees came from eleven different countries, and in his inaugural speech on values Ma declared that only with a "common sense of values" could such a disparate group of people be able to "unite and fight toward tomorrow." He then cited an example from the Song dynasty, a story well known to Chinese about the heroes at Mount Liang, the stronghold of the 108 legendary heroes of *Outlaws of the Marsh*. "The mission of the One Hundred and Eight was to implement the *dao* [the Way] on behalf of heaven. No matter what happened, they were brothers in that endeavor." This reference was drawn from the historical bandit Song Jiang and his outlaw companions from medieval times. (Song Jiang surrendered to government troops in 1119; Robin Hood is said to have died in Yorkshire in around 1247, and the legends of both are similar.)

A code of honor served as the primary bond for both Song Jiang and Robin Hood's bandits. In elevating the moral mission of his employees, Jack Ma similarly wanted to create strong cohesion by getting employees to assimilate specific value concepts. By now, Alibaba's Six Values are factored into annual employee evaluations, so they form a rigorous part of each person's thinking. Employees are not allowed to think of them as vague concepts. These values have become the criteria for measuring performance, which to a large degree has molded the corporate culture of Alibaba; they are the yardstick in figuring out which people to hire, how to train them, how to test them, who moves up, and who moves out.

This concept was to be vital as the company absorbed employees from Yahoo! China. In August 2005, Yahoo! China and Alibaba formed a strategic partnership that involved a transfer of $1 billion to Alibaba as well as hundreds of employees. On September 21, 2005, the Z9 train from Beijing to Hangzhou was turned into a private express for Alibaba. It brought some six hundred Yahoo! people down to Hangzhou to meet the rest of their new "family" in advance of the official formalization of the deal the next month. During the welcoming ceremonies, Alibaba raised a huge banner on which was written a message about being "one family." Merging corporate cultures is generally the hardest part of combining forces; Ma was determined to make this union work, and he gave a speech that indicated his emphasis on corporate culture.

I have been working in Beijing for much of August, partly because I wanted to hear what colleagues had to say and partly to make sure that they heard what I had to say. So that they could understand me. Understanding me is pretty easy, but it does not mean that you understand Alibaba. Alibaba is a team, not just me, and it has a strong culture. We have always been in Hangzhou, which means that the outside world does not understand us too well. I don't mean just foreigners but also people in China. When people look at Alibaba, therefore, they think it's all Jack Ma. I feel badly about that. In fact, this company is the result of a lot of hard work of a whole team of superb people. I'm just the one who does all the talking, I'm the spokesman. When I went to Beijing, everyone could see and understand me, but what they really need to do is understand this company and its team, understand the corporate culture, and also understand Hangzhou. Alibaba's future is inseparable from Hangzhou. So I wanted to have everyone come down here and see it for themselves. This is extremely important. We are talking about the environment in which the company has grown, and the linking of cultures and place. All of these are living, breathing things, not just things that Ma talks about. I brought you here to make sure you feel this company, experience this city, understand the climate in which we operate.

Back in Beijing, Ma also spoke at the Great Hall of the People on September 23, addressing twenty-five hundred Alibaba employees, now joined by another seven hundred "relatives" from Yahoo! China.

Trust

In addition to a focus on values in terms of employee behavior, Ma has placed a strong emphasis on trust as the only effective way to do business in the long term. This trust does not mean some kind of touchy-feely faith in human nature. Quite the opposite: Ma has institutionalized trust by putting in place a series of measures for authenticating and verifying the background of any enterprise on Alibaba. He began this process in March 2002, with what he called a Trust Zone for China Suppliers. This was done in cooperation with credit management companies in China. This process of supplying credit ratings and verification and authentication services allowed Alibaba to surge forward in its B2B business.

Ma feels that what determines the success or failure of B2B is not funding or technology but something much more important: the simple consideration of trustworthiness. As a result, he has focused on systems that allow small and medium-sized enterprises to operate in a "safety zone." Both sides in any transaction have to be able to see the credentials of the other side, whether these be corporate documentation, legal decisions, volume of business on Alibaba, or ranking by other members. Alibaba buys the services of a number of credit-rating companies for its domestic suppliers. Foreign club members must pass through an evaluation by such professional institutions as Dun & Bradstreet before being allowed entry.

"Only trustworthy people are able to get rich," is Ma's slogan. Alibaba began to charge a fee for such services in October 2000. The fee for club membership is currently $385 (RMB 2,800) per year for China TrustPass members. For so-called Gold Suppliers on the international marketplace, the membership fee is $5,500 to $8,200 (RMB 40,000–60,000), depending on services provided. Gold Supplier members currently total twenty-two thousand, while International TrustPass members, a kind of incubator for the Gold Supplier products, total eleven thousand. Membership has risen, not declined, with the rise in prices, and this is because members actually make money from the services they are provided. Ma regards the number of members and the volume of business that they are able to do through Alibaba as his core asset. "This is the mountain at my back," he says. "This is my security, my support."

To reinforce the idea that Alibaba is a team with a strong corporate culture and that its strength is the bottom-line satisfaction it gives to customers, he has hung behind his desk a photograph of all employees above this statement: "We created Alibaba." Near it is the couplet calligraphed by his friend Louis Cha. Ma adheres closely to the concept of taking very practical steps to achieve Alibaba aims. He takes it as the core of his management practices.

Jack Ma (right) and Jerry Yang (co-founder of Yahoo!), photographed on the Great Wall together in 1998. Ma and his colleagues had not yet founded Alibaba at the time.

At the end of 1999, Jack Ma and the boss of Softbank, Masayoshi Son, signed an agreement giving Alibaba a much-needed initial investment. Son, ethnically Chinese but of Korean heritage and born in Japan, recognized a kindred spirit in the rebellious Ma.

Jack Ma and colleagues on a rare outing to the Great Wall in 1999. Ma and his early core team were working for a subsidiary of the Ministry of Foreign Economic Relations and Trade at the time. This photo preceded their return to Hangzhou and was taken at a time when the future seemed bleak.

President Bill Clinton attended the Fifth Swordplay Conference in China and was photographed with Jack Ma in Hangzhou on September 10, 2005.

The SARS crisis erupted in early spring 2003. This photo shows Ma and his Alibaba employees during a tough period. Company solidarity and high morale allowed business to carry on, even though Alibaba was under strict quarantine at the time.

中国 😊 下一浪
媒体见面会【杭州】二零零三年十一月
主办单位：西湖论剑大会组委会
承办单位：阿里巴巴
Alibaba.com

西湖论剑

Young entrepreneurs at the Fourth Swordplay Conference, held in 2003. The backdrop reads, "China: The Next Wave." From left to right, the people in the photo are Liang Jianzhang, CEO of Ctrip.com (an online travel company), Ma Yun (Jack Ma), Wang Leilei, president of the Tom.com Group, and Li Zhenhong, president of Baidu Company.

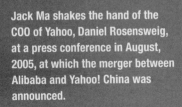

Jack Ma shakes the hand of the COO of Yahoo, Daniel Rosensweig, at a press conference in August, 2005, at which the merger between Alibaba and Yahoo! China was announced.

Jack Ma is famous for waving his hands in the air as he speaks, perhaps the legacy of parents who were professional performers of "Ping Tan," the Suzhou storytelling tradition. Ma grew up among dramatic communicators. His personal vigor and motivational speeches are part of what have propelled the company forward.

In 2006, Ma was honored with an award called the Yangzi River Delta Award. It recognizes entrepreneurial achievement and specifically awards the leadership of innovative young people.

Jack Ma giving a sign of confidence as he sits under the Alibaba and Taobao banners, visual representations of the empire he has created.

Taobao: A New Weapon in Jack Ma's Arsenal

n May 2003, a notice appeared on Alibaba's internal Web site that seemed to warn employees about a fast-developing Web site called Taobao. The notice said, "Attention, a group of people are quickly creating a site very similar to Alibaba, but for individual consumers. It's name is Taobao." Debate began immediately inside the company about this new threat. People were soon talking about nothing else in their spare time, but senior management appeared unaware of the problem and remained mute.

Alibaba employees began to get angry, wondering why management did not investigate this looming problem. In July, Alibaba announced that it was investing $12 million (RMB 100 million) to create China's biggest personal transaction site in China: Taobao. Only after this announcement did employees realize that Taobao was their very own child.

In Chinese the word *taobao* means "searching or prospecting for treasure." Ma had maintained tight secrecy in the course of developing this gold-panning idea. Work had begun around the time of the SARS crisis in the spring of 2003 and had continued offsite, unknown to all but a few in the company. Corporate cohesion and a degree of secrecy unknown to most organizations in China is one of Jack Ma's strengths. He considers organizational structure to be a part of the company's technology and its reason for success. Employees are required to maintain strict confidentiality about organizational structure. "Our structure is our core competitiveness. It has been hammered out over the course of many mistakes," says Ma. "I myself don't know how Sina is organized and run. If I did know, it would be easy to attack and defeat them."

On April 7, 2003, Ma had called together about ten Alibaba employees in an urgent meeting. They were asked to sign nondisclosure statements; this was not forced upon them but was meant to impress on them the need for secrecy. All did in fact sign the statements, which one employee later noted "were totally in English so we had no time to read and absorb the whole thing anyway." After the meeting, this core group was transferred to the original Lakeside Garden rooms, the "sacred land" of Alibaba, where work had first begun. There they worked on the development of the new site. "At first, we were just wanting to maintain secrecy, so we separated out the group," Ma said later. When SARS hit, however, the separation proved to be fortuitous, as the group was able to continue intensive and undisturbed work.

Taobao soon became legendary in the field of C2C auction marketplaces inside China. It started from a base of zero and in the short space of two years had become the number one on-line auction mart in the country. This was not unrelated to the strength of the company from which it had been spawned, but the development of Taobao nonetheless represented an enormous risk. It was a gamble that could have taken Alibaba out of action: Jack Ma essentially mortgaged Alibaba in order to bring Taobao into being.

Ma is a natural gambler, with an acute sense of the market. When Alibaba announced that it would be putting serious money into developing Taobao, winter shadows were still darkening the skies of the Internet world. Alibaba's investment represented the largest sum invested by a China company in Internet activity since the bursting of the dot-com bubble. Moreover, Taobao had strong competition. Foreign-owned eBay had purchased one-third of the shares of a Chinese company called EachNet in 2002 for $30 million, and in 2003 eBay purchased the remaining shares for $150 million. The combined eBay-EachNet site held 80 percent of market share, and eBay had vowed to continue investing in the China market in order to maintain absolute dominance.

Jack Ma's decision to enter the C2C realm was dubbed a "reckless gamble" by all media at the time. Meg Whitman, global head of eBay, forecast that "Taobao will survive at most for eighteen months." Eighteen months later, eBay had to revise that forecast. Zheng Xigui, eBay's COO in China, announced instead, "We are preparing to fight a protracted war in China; we are ready to go forward with a one-hundred-year plan." Gone was the assurance of easy victory. By now, Meg Whitman herself had left eBay, leaving the situation in China for Li Ka-shing and Tom. com to sort out.

The term *move* in martial arts parlance appropriately characterizes Jack Ma's strategy in this instance. Mongolian wrestlers may circle each other for an hour before one makes a lightning-fast move and the other is suddenly on the ground. The Chinese boxer Hu Qing weighs less than 110 pounds, but the speed and timing of his thrust is teaching the sport that the right move can easily overcome muscle. Ma's move came in the form of a fiendish decision: without warning, he decided to allow users on Taobao to conduct transactions for free. This was the closest thing he could do to "kneecapping" eBay, which was already charging a fee. The Internet culture of China is different from that of the United States: Ma knew that eBay-EachNet's user fees were the cause of such customer complaints that they were an Achilles' heel for eBay in China. "Alibaba kept to the idea of growing the market first. We knew we couldn't and shouldn't try to make money right away." As a result of this policy, eBay-EachNet saw its customer base irrevocably melt away.

Alibaba's strategy had been planned well in advance. The idea was born in early 2003, when Alibaba's business was relatively stable and Ma felt that the consumer e-commerce marketplace was beginning to mature. The senior manager Sun Danyu was put in charge of the Taobao project. Sun remembers that "eBay-EachNet had become quite large in China, but we recognized that it had a lot of weaknesses too. Customers complained, which was our opportunity. The complaints were directed at the payment fees. They were an inappropriate strategy for China at the time."

Western companies such as Amazon.com, in addition to eBay, have adhered to a business model that charges a percentage fee for each transaction. The model has enabled companies to bring in a measure of revenue and not simply give away the digital "farm." China's Alibaba and Taobao believed that transactions should be free, at least initially, while services enable them to charge an overall membership fee. Additional value-added services can be selected off a menu, depending on need. That model works well under certain conditions: a company must have enough capital to survive the period before reaching critical mass, and a company must have a large and effective sales force in order to grow membership fast. Taobao had both of these qualifications.

Preparations were intense before launching Taobao. Having pinpointed the opponent's weak points, Sun Danyu completed a detailed market research and strategic plan in just 120 days, down to the composition of the founding team of ten people. The team went to work in secrecy and emerged with a product. With no market promotion of any kind, Taobao was formally launched on May 10, 2003. Within the next twenty days, Taobao had received its ten thousandth registered customer.

Bloodbath in the Advertising Arena

Profits are the weathervane for businessmen. At the same time, the Chinese believe that if you have enough capital, in a market economy you can generally fight your way into most businesses before you turn a profit. Fighting one's way into a new market for Alibaba required massive investment, though, particularly in advertising and promotion. Products not advertised are, as they say in China, like the suggestive glances of a hopeful lover on a pitch-black night: they get nowhere.

When Taobao was launched, Alibaba was therefore already fighting its way forward under the protective shield of a heavy advertising budget. By the end of July 2004, its competitor in the B2B market, Huicong, had burned through close to $1.2 million (RMB 10 million) in advertising with the clear objective of skewering its opponent. Alibaba, for its part, now put several million into ads on television. "We will not spare any funds," responded Huicong. "We will continue the advertising war against Alibaba to the end."

In the C2C realm, the fighting was worse. Advertising wars within China had become violently competitive. Alibaba had decided to advertise Taobao on the Internet but soon came up against concerted opposition: eBay had signed exclusive advertising agreements with the three main portals in China. The agreements stated that if these portals were found to be doing promotion of any kind with competitors of eBay, they would pay large fines. At this point eBay defined its competitors as including the various auction sites of Ya-bao, Yibi-de, Guardian Online, Yahoo! Auction, and Taobao. With little recourse, Taobao was forced to place ads in such ignominious locations as subway stations, public buses, and elevators.

"In order to increase name recognition of Taobao," Sun Danyu stated, "we will be spending in the neighborhood of several tens of millions of RMB in ads." Despite this bravado, people in the company knew that the best promotion was in fact word of mouth. Far more registered members have come into the auction site via this method than any other. The conventional wisdom had been that advertising on portals was the best medium for C2C advertising. Faced with a blockade by the portals, Taobao found other ways and in the process discovered that they worked better. The Taobao advertising strategy involved three stages. The first was to rely completely on word-of-mouth communication, which brought an early group of users into the site. These members were important in laying the foundation for the next stage in Taobao's growth, that of the "farming villages surround the cities" strategy. Harking back to a guerrilla tactic in warfare, the phrase in this context meant using SMS (short message service) Web sites that badly needed revenue since they had recently been hurt by tightening government policies. The third stage came from the end of 2003 to the beginning of 2004, when Taobao was able to set up a cooperative relationship with MSN China. At the time, several other Internet companies bid more than Taobao for this alliance, but MSN chose Taobao for strategic reasons.

Through all of these methods, Taobao was able to break out of the embargo placed upon it by the three main portals. It found a number of breaches in eBay's wall. All of these experiences sharpened the skills and toughened the willpower of both the Alibaba and the Taobao teams. Like their leader, they seemed to thrive on adversity. Like him, too, they found ways around problems and discovered that when one's opponent is doing one thing it is the best time to do another.

Taobao, Alipay, and Localization

Mencius, a venerated Chinese philosopher, noted, "Climate, geography, and man must be in accord." This saying, dating from around 300 B.C.E., expresses a tenet that is equally true today.

The word in Chinese for *localization* uses the character for "earth," and signifies "being of the local earth." Only by being rooted in local circumstances in China can one hope to sweep away all obstacles, and make oneself invincible. There is in fact no other way to do business in China, for local circumstances are very much under local control. Few foreign enterprises in China have fully been able to master all the problems in being local, to "win over the spirits of the local water and earth." They recognize the issues in theory but find it hard to implement them in practice. Localization requires the understanding that companies both benefit from and must in turn contribute to the local soil in which they grow. Chinese companies are well aware that they exist in a society that must benefit from their activities: they pay attention to cultivating that society.

The Chinese phrase that is often used to describe this nurturing activity can be interpreted in many ways. To Western minds, "Gathering together resources from the four directions, which allows one to create benefit for the eight realms" may sound abstruse, but it is quite concrete in the Chinese context. In general, it means that a company has to be in accord with "all under heaven," which means making sure that the company does not benefit alone. The long-term way of business is through people's hearts, it is not through short-term profit and opportunistic self-interest. It also involves, therefore, intricate (and perhaps to the Western mind unseemly) interrelationships between government and corporate business. To the Chinese, however, these interrelationships are simply an integral part of the cultivation of local soil. Taobao understood these things.

Prior to beginning the strategy by which he countered eBay, Jack Ma liked to say that "eBay may be a shark in the ocean, but we are a crocodile in the Yangtze River. We will be defeated if we fight out on the open seas. If we fight here in the river, there's no chance they are going to win." He knew what he was talking about—in terms of local support, nobody has a stronger position than Jack Ma. While eBay was going for globalization, Taobao was deciding to play the opposite hand: it would be relying on extreme localization and on the resources of its native soil. Ma often reminds his team that it is useful to change your stance frequently in order to see things from different perspectives. Taobao in effect changed its global stance, went local, and as a result, so far at least, has won the game.

Although eBay may have understood these things equally well, it had difficulty complying with the rules of the game. Two key problems for eBay were its need, as a publicly owned company, to show profits, and its inability, as an American company, to operate a viable payment platform without full regulatory assistance. In America, the business model of eBay has worked spectacularly well; eBay realized profits almost from the beginning and for years has delivered excellent annual results. It has become one of the fastest-growing enterprises in the world. Trying to copy this miracle in China has been another story. Without being carefully attuned to the Chinese concept of "climate, geography, and man," eBay had a near-zero chance of success. In its defense, eBay played a very good game. China's consumer e-commerce market had been dominated by the Internet-based transaction platform known as EachNet; eBay first invested in and then bought this company. All the way up to early 2006, this company played the dominant role in China's C2C market. Somebody calculated that the volume of business transacted on EachNet in 2003 was roughly equivalent to the total 2003 sales volume of ten Wal-Mart stores inside China. According to the chairman and CEO of eBay-EachNet, Shao Yipo, three million people bought things on eBay-EachNet every day. More than thirty-five thousand types of things were traded: e-Bay-EachNet's sellers sold a national flag every five minutes in China, a watch every three minutes, a stamp-collecting item every minute, a pair of athletic shoes every thirty seconds, and a T-shirt every ten seconds. With EachNet, eBay had a strong position until Taobao's superior staying power and regulatory support undercut its business.

Taobao knew the unique considerations in China and prepared for the challenge. Preparations required building up a large war chest and engineering entire systems that did not exist before. To resolve the secure-payment-system bottleneck, Taobao developed Alipay. Just as Alibaba had incubated Taobao, so Taobao incubated Alipay. It now is a separately incorporated company, but from the beginning Alipay enjoyed the support of a China-first regulatory policy in the area of online payment.

Unlike Taobao, eBay was not an insider and did not enjoy the same freedom to utilize government-supported payment systems. Regulatory restrictions are key to creating a barrier to foreign entry in the financial and communications arenas in China. The fact that Alibaba is headquartered abroad is immaterial: creative licensing enables the company to stay under the protective wing of China's regulatory system, a native son on native ground.

"We Do Not Intend to Make a Profit for the Next Three Years"

In conventional wisdom, a company that does not make a profit is a company that will not survive. Only if you have profits will you have investors, and only *then* can you really grow. Shareholders, employees, the enterprise itself—all depend on this basic understanding.

Jack Ma went against this mainstream thinking with Taobao. He determined that Taobao would be a completely free service for at least its first year and would not expect any profits for its first three years. In China, as elsewhere, this was called "burning money," and most people disapproved of the method. Only one who both saw farther down the road and had the resources to survive could play this game. Ma had figured it out in detail in advance. He did not hide his intentions: he calmly stated, "The reason we have saved up such a hoard of cash is so that we can go out and wage war."

The target of that war was eBay. The war was waged against a company that had been cultivating the market for several years and was just beginning to taste the sweetness of making some money. The Taobao warning was clear: if eBay-EachNet did not similarly implement a free policy, many of its customers would be moving to Taobao.

With Taobao, Ma did not intend to keep losing money forever. Based on his calculations, he simply believed that a circuitous path to the goal was best. Ma was not only striking out at eBay in implementing a free policy, however. He was accepting reality. Unlike eBay's managers, Ma recognized that the time was not ripe in China for charging fees for a service that couldn't sustain them. If under a fee-based business model you did not in fact win customers and did not in fact make a profit, then you were hastening your demise by charging fees. On the other hand, if for a period you could build up a loyal base of customers, satisfy their needs, and begin to be necessary to their own profitability, then you could blithely charge fees in the future. Ma believed that in the future Taobao absolutely would be profitable. "We have a sufficient amount of 'deep breath' to hold us," Ma told his team, drawing on the analogy of *qigong* practice. "And we have plenty of confidence. After all, before Alibaba began to charge fees it also went through a three-year stage of free services."

As a result of this, up to now, not one of Taobao's departments faces the pressure of having to be a profit center. The goal of the operating department of the Web site is to make a site that is as simple and easy to use as possible, and to make club members feel comfortable and at ease. The goal of the technical department is to make the site stable and secure for purchasing. The PR department is asked to popularize the whole concept of Web purchasing, to spread the practice throughout the general Chinese public. Meanwhile, the finance department is asked to keep tabs. As Ma says, "We know the difference between spending money and burning money. We also know that we are making a choice between putting our energies toward making a tiny amount of money right now and putting our energies toward creating channels for water to flow into in the future." *Water* is a synonym for *money* in China.

Taobao has a well-developed timetable for its staged development and for the day it intends to start turning a profit. This is not emphasized to employees, however. They are not to waste their time worrying about it. Ma often says, "If a person's mind is always counting money, worried about money, he will never be able to satisfy the real needs of customers. He won't be putting the customer first." The corollary: only when Taobao club members are making money themselves will Taobao itself and its employees be making money. As with Alibaba, Ma emphasizes that the first five dollars in a member's pocket should stay there and help him make fifty dollars. Only then should Taobao reach in and ask for five.

The Strategy Sounds Good; Will It Work?

China's manufacturing industries are currently facing increasingly thin profit margins, their level of discomfort is rising, and in general things are perceived to be getting worse. Inflation is rising rapidly, higher costs of inputs are forcing price increases and slower sales, and the common man is feeling the pinch. Faced with this, Chinese businesses are being forced to be inventive and find better models. This is part of what spurred Jack Ma and Taobao to break the old B2C mold.

The traditional B2C business model requires a large investment in warehouses and distribution centers. Middleman costs are high, and the profit margin generally remains around 5 percent. Jack Ma is not in favor of traditional B2C models—for good reason. He feels that, "even in America, with its excellent logistical systems, a company like Amazon is only making 5 percent. In China, the B2C market is fairly mature, but look at Joyo and Dangdang—they are finding it hard, which says to me that the model has problems." As a result, on May 10, 2006, Alibaba announced that the largest Internet-based marketplace in Asia, Taobao, was formally launching a completely new kind of B2C enterprise. It declared that the Taobao B2C model was different from the traditional model as represented by Amazon.

Back in 2004, Ma had already indicated that e-commerce would not have the same distinctions between B2B and B2C—the lines would be blurred. "Like running water, which you just reach out and use these days, buying things on the Internet will be the same. It will be that convenient." At the same time, Ma has predicted that in the future all forms of e-commerce will converge, operating on top of a large platform. After linking up the previous platforms, a completely new form of B2C model will be born.

In 2005 Ma began to test this idea. He led Alibaba's buyers and sellers over to Taobao and encouraged Taobao sellers to put product on Alibaba. He was seeing if the companies could indeed break through the barrier between B2B and C2C, cross-fertilizing and thus increasing the total market.

Sun Danyu has commented on a process that both he and Jack Ma feel will be the way business is handled in the future. "The traditional profit model for B2C involves putting pressure on producers to lower their prices, and thereby taking a larger margin between the buying price and the selling price. The new B2C model helps the seller be the actual seller. The platform itself is paid for its service; it is not taking a margin for the transaction." This critical difference means that the B2C service is an ally who is stroking the fur in the right direction, making everybody want the same thing. As Sun explains, "Our services model allows product producers to keep more profit, which in the end means that they put more resources into technology and innovation. In the end, that allows the great mass of consumers to benefit as well." Sun adds, "The purpose of Taobao's model is to help factory producers make money and to help consumers save money. It is to shorten the chain between ultimate buyer and ultimate seller, including all those links along the way that take up money."

This model had been gestating in Alibaba for a long time. The company knew that it required a host of supporting roles from affiliated organizations: banks, credit organizations, authentication and verification services, payment platforms, security and credit-rating firms. Only with the development of an entire system could the innovative power of enterprises that Sun eulogized finally reach out to benefit consumers. All the various parts of a complex system had to be nudged forward simultaneously for the model to fly. Several factors have worked in Alibaba's favor, including the export-driven model of China's fast-growing economy.

Storefronts is the term used to describe the main way producers make their presence and products known on both the Alibaba and Taobao platforms. Ma has said that in fact Alibaba and Taobao operate as online real estate companies, providing services to companies that situate themselves along their "roads." As soon as the new Taobao model appeared, a number of well-known brands, both international and Chinese, began setting up dedicated storefronts on Taobao. Major brands routinely using the site today include Motorola, Nokia, Haier, Lenovo, Great Wall Computer, Apple iPod, and many others. Some companies have begun making products specifically for the Taobao B2C platform. As of June 2007, Alibaba.com hosted 2.4 million storefronts. This should be seen in the context of there being only around 1.5 million Web sites in China. Of the storefronts, 22,000 paid for Gold Supplier status and 10,900 for International TrustPass status on the international marketplace; 222,000 paid for China TrustPass status on the domestic marketplace. Taobao's statistics, including revenue and profit figures, are less available than Alibaba.com's, given that the company is still closely held.

Even as Taobao's storefronts increased, various other players were positioning themselves. According to Shao Yipo, eBay-EachNet's CEO, eBay was extremely pleased to be investing even more in EachNet. Within fifteen years, eBay predicted, China's market would become the largest individual online marketplace in the world.

Jack Ma heard all this, and he must have smiled. He sat there biding his time, with a massive amount of cash in his back pocket. He knew that sometimes you had to be patient, but he was ready to take the gamble. Ma waited, and in the meantime invested another $42 million (RMB 350 million) in Taobao.

Forming Alliances: The Three Big Portals and the Three Big Auction Houses

Although Ma is independent by nature, he has never rejected the benefits of forming strategic alliances when it serves a business purpose. He knows that, like his heroes, one is not fully in control of one's own fate.

Faced with greater foreign competition as a result of WTO regulations, many Chinese companies have been gathering in protective groups, which are given different names, such as "group," "alliance," or "partnership," depending on the situation. Several industries enjoy special consideration due to national security factors, including media, publishing, banking and finance, and the Internet, but they too will face a day of reckoning in the near future. Alibaba began to recognize that a strategic alliance would be in its interests as the competition heated up. Ma is aware that forming an alliance is an art form: it requires matching up the synergies of appropriate partners and avoiding traps, but in this case, he had to take the risk, for others were recognizing the same logic. Since the early 2000s , the field of players has been shifting and reconfiguring: Sina allied with Yahoo! and NetEase came to an agreement with EachNet, while Sohu allied itself with Taobao.

The NetEase-EachNet affiliation is one unfortunate proof

of how hard it is to make such alliances stick. The two companies were initially optimistic about prospects, and NetEase's CEO, Li Jinghui, and EachNet's CEO, Shao Yipo, were full of smiles. The cooperation did not last long. On July 9, 2002, a crack appeared in the alliance when a link to NetEase's own auction house showed up on the homepage of NetEase. This apparently unethical move was disturbing to the industry, as EachNet declared that NetEase was copying EachNet's site, and initiated legal action. In the end, an out-of-court settlement calmed things down, but both parties were left with ill feelings. The result? EachNet and eBay formed a strategic relationship in March 2002. In June 2003, eBay increased its investment in China by acquiring EachNet.

Taobao and Sohu Link Up

On April 12, 2005, Sohu and Taobao (now China's largest consumer auction site) announced that they too were forming a strategic alliance. Both enjoyed a large customer user base. They agreed to cooperate both online and off in promoting the advance of China's Internet-based economy.

This time, the two really did become strategic alliance partners and were able to realize the potential of the union. Sogo, under Sohu, was one of the best-known Internet brands in China, with tens of millions of registered users and tremendous traffic; its contents and search capabilities were unique. Taobao also enjoyed superior brand recognition and premier technology. The chairman of the board and CEO of Sohu, Zhang Chaoyang, expressed his optimism about this cooperation with Taobao. "This is providing a completely new cooperative model for the C2C industry," he declared. "Cooperating with Taobao provides Sohu's tremendous user base an arena for secure online transactions, which will help spur the development of e-commerce. In addition, payment questions have always troubled Chinese e-commerce; we are glad to see the launching of Alipay, a tool that is providing new methods of resolving the bottleneck of secure payment for Internet transactions. We will continue to pay close attention to Alipay and will look for ways to cooperate in the future."

In April 2005 Ma said, "Taobao is China's largest C2C Web site. It enjoys nearly 5.3 million registered members at present [that figure would increase dramatically to 39.9 million by the end of June 2007] and more than 6 million trade items. Taobao respects the leading position of Sohu in the world of portals, and admires its strong positioning in the market." Taobao's COO, Sun Danyu, analyzed the way the situation had changed over the years: "China's Internet has transitioned from merely trying to get the attention of browsers and providing them with entertainment toward recognizing that the Net must be useful and must provide businesses with tools to grow. Our alliance is another indication of a maturing industry."

Two Dragons Fight for the Pearl

The world has many examples of two dragons fighting for a pearl: Coca-Cola and Pepsi, McDonald's and KFC. In China, when there is talk about eBay, people generally mention Taobao in the same breath: despite their realignment, the two continue to be heated contenders for the online auction marketplace. At first, this seems to be comparing apples and oranges, for until recently Taobao has not come close to being in the same class as the global giant eBay. Any direct challenge against eBay would have been foolhardy. From today's perspective, however, eBay seems to have been all but chased out of China, and Jack Ma can sit back and smile.

In December 2006, eBay bowed to the reality of its diminished role in China and announced a joint venture with the TOM Group to carry forward operations. The TOM Group is one of the leading Chinese-language media groups in the greater China region and is controlled by the tycoon Li Ka-shing. According to the official press release regarding this new venture, "eBay will have a 49 percent stake in the joint venture, and TOM Online [a subsidiary of TOM Group] will have a 51 percent stake. Both companies will make financial contributions to the venture, including a US$40 million cash contribution from eBay and US$20 million in financing from TOM Online."

The Seemingly No-Move Move: Alibaba's Competitive Advantage

For an Internet company to become first in its industry in two years and the largest consumer online marketplace in China is notable. Each of Taobao's actions has also, intentionally or not, influenced the overall industry in China. Taobao is called a miracle in the history of the China Internet.

In looking at this miracle, *Forbes* magazine has written, "If Jack Ma has his way, then his will be the company dominating the global online auction marketplace, not eBay, but Taobao." How did Taobao manage to pull down the company everyone considered to be invincible, and in so little time? Jack Ma's answer is the same as it has always been: "Only through conscientious service can Taobao be universally acclaimed. Only through conscientious service can one win a customer's satisfaction and trust. This is the path to growth for any enterprise."

Alibaba provides service in e-commerce, as a B2B online business services company. It manages and operates the globe's largest

Internet-based trading marketplace. Every day, Alibaba's Web site has on it products from more than 220 countries and regions. It uses the "ecosystem" that the company has built: the TrustPass services, the Gold Supplier services, the storefront building services, the payment platform, and others. The key consideration determining Alibaba's survival is its ongoing level of quality of service.

In order to ensure that Alibaba users were satisfied, Ma brought over a new concept from the home electronics company Haier. This was called the "one piece of fabric" concept, and it was used successfully at Haier. When its servicepeople first started going into people's homes to install an air conditioner or refrigerator, they would bring with them a piece of fabric with which they would wipe up their tracks before they left. This simple gesture of respect made people so happy that it became a very effective sales tool. This polite service strategy of Haier was adapted to Alibaba's circumstances. Its underlying concept is an attitude of total service. Taobao was the beneficiary of all these Alibaba strategies for success. Most importantly, it benefited from Alipay. If no fees and a trust-evaluation system enabled Taobao to develop its base, the decisive factor in allowing the company to grow has been Alipay's method of secure payment. Trust is the treasure by which Taobao has routed eBay, but the contribution of Alipay has been indispensable.

In May 2006, the China Internet Network Information Center (CNNIC) released a report on the consumer online transaction market. Taobao held 67.3 percent of market share, greatly exceeding eBay-EachNet's 29.1 percent. The number of Taobao users had reached 19 million, slightly lower than eBay-EachNet's 20.5 million but rising fast. By December 2006, eBay was forced to admit that Taobao's business model had essentially crippled its competitiveness in China. Carefully declaring that it was *not* pulling out of China, it sought a "big mountain at its back" in the form of Li Ka-shing. It conceded majority ownership in the country to his TOM Group.

Taobao had indeed been a gamble, but as of 2008, its revenues were growing 100 percent year after year, and it is the largest consumer marketplace in China. Its main competitor is now TOM EachNet, jointly owned 49 percent by eBay and 51 percent by the TOM Group. A second and serious competitor is Paipai. com, a company owned by Tencent and whose name signifies an auction market. It is assumed that eventually Taobao will start charging for listings or transactions; until that time, it continues to scoop in customers, all of whom bring cross-platform benefits for the other Alibaba businesses. They use Alipay for payment, and many Taobao sellers actually source their products on Alibaba. com's domestic marketplace.

By the time of Taobao's ascent, Alipay had already completed seamless payment arrangements with the four major state-owned banks of China, as well as the China Merchant Bank system; it will likely be a good horse to follow in the future. Taobao moved up to being number one in China within two years of its founding. This so-called miracle of Taobao is easier to understand when one remembers that the company is still not, in fact, making money.

Alipay: A New Milestone in E-Commerce

W all Street has predicted that whoever holds the initiative in online payment systems will control China's e-commerce markets. That entity may well be Alipay, an affiliate of the umbrella Alibaba Group. Alipay is currently the largest online payment platform in China and is similar in most respects to PayPal in the United States. It has more than fifty-eight million active users and over three hundred thousand merchants accepting the service. It has close contractual relations with China's largest banks. It is owned and controlled by the Alibaba Group. The company is in that new and nebulous region of Internet banking and finance that is witness to the rapid convergence of financial and information industries.

The original idea behind Alipay was that it should serve as an escrow service for buyer and seller: it would serve as guarantor between parties to a transaction, by holding funds until products were actually received. Now expanding that limited role, Alipay is beginning to offer loans to customers on the basis of their credit rating, which in turn is partly based on their volume of online transactions. It has ties with Visa, so overseas customers can pay or be paid online easily. It is morphing into a very powerful entity, one that is not under the scrutiny of the Alibaba.com stock market listing. E-commerce requires cooperation with large commercial banks, in addition to very substantial back-office technical support. In the present environment in China, Alipay's ability to resolve the payment security issues is a significant breakthrough in China's e-commerce business.

Monetizing transactions via Alipay is one of Alibaba's best opportunities for evolving its business. Daily transactions in recent months are in the neighborhood of 1 million to 1.2 million, with peak daily payment volume of over $4 million (RMB 250 million). Alibaba.com earns a revenue share of between 60 percent and 85 percent of the transaction amount for cross-selling services. The parent group owns Alipay, but if registered users of Alibaba.com pay each other with Alipay, then Alibaba.com receives 60 percent to 85 percent of the consequent fees. This effectively monetizes transactions.

The banking field estimates that Alipay facilitated more than $4.5 billion (RMB 35 billion) of transactions involving individual consumers in 2007. Payment between parties at a distance from each other is a ready source of income to the company; payment systems involving closer parties are more intractable, since competition includes all the conventional modes of payment. In the online arena, competitors are PayPal China, Chinapay, Tenpay (owned by Tencent), and UMpay (owned by TOM Online). One excellent asset of Alipay is its good relationship with financial regulators and commercial banks. The company works closely with these to ensure its systems are timely, hassle free, government-facilitated in the sense of approved licenses, and inexpensive.

As a system, Taobao is enabled by Alipay. A number of surveys have shown that users know the benefits of purchasing on the Internet but remain concerned about the security of payment. The effectiveness of security systems in the course of transactions is key. Jack Ma agrees that there can be no true e-commerce in China without resolving payment security problems, and he also knows that resolving customer concerns will lead to an explosion of China's e-commerce. When customers are fully comfortable, Taobao will begin to make serious money. To guarantee transaction security, Ma has established several layers of security on top of the Taobao system. Any seller first has to receive a certificate of authentication and verification from the Public Security Bureau of China. Every seller is ranked in a trustworthiness ranking system, which includes volume of business done through the system and other safeguards.

Statistics indicate that one in ten thousand transactions on Taobao leads to problems, a ratio that approaches the level in Europe and the United States. In America, the average amount of money lost to swindlers in an Internet transaction is said to be $293; in China, it is less but the overall problem is worse, given the many links in the chain of any transaction and the less sophisticated state of the infrastructure. Recognizing that security and trustworthiness are key, Ma has long since cultivated a kind of Scotland Yard–like operation within his company, which independently investigates problems. The names of the employees are confidential, for the safety of family members, but available material suggests they are highly trained professionals in the field of investigation. In one known case, a person who swindled a buyer was apprehended less than fifteen minutes after withdrawing the transferred funds from his bank account.

At least three e-commerce companies have set up secure-payment platforms in recent years: EachNet was first in launching its Easy Payment Pass service back in 2000. After that, Alibaba set up TrustPass, and Huicong set up Buyer's Business Pass, although these did not include all features of safe payment. Taobao experimentally launched the Alipay service on October 18, 2003. In the short space of one year it achieved fairly good results, and it has since become the premier payment platform in China.

The system continues to work as a kind of escrow account, in which banks hold a buyer's funds until products have been received. The basic transaction process is as follows: (1) the buyer selects the product, (2) the buyer remits funds to Alipay, (3) Alipay notifies the seller to issue goods, (4) the seller issues the goods to the buyer, (5) the buyer receives the goods and notifies Alipay, (6) Alipay releases the funds to the seller, and (7) the transaction is completed. As with any credit card used for a transaction, the buyer is first evaluated in an authentication and verification process. Other value-added services include the ability to track funds, manage inquiries, and handle accounts.

Directly using a credit card for online payment in China increases the risk of losing control of one's funds, but Alipay has basically resolved this security issue. Within a few seconds, payment can be made in a safe and easy manner. In this Internet era, an Alipay account is a kind of electronic purse.

No Thieves on Earth: The Taobao Version

In 2004 and 2005, Taobao rode the wave of a popular television show in China called *No Thieves on Earth*. The plot involved a male thief and his female accomplice, and two pickpockets called Wang Bao and Wang Li. On a train, the two meet up with a farmer, appropriately called Foolish Bumpkin. Bumpkin is just returning from the big city, where he has been able to make a pile of money. He is looking forward to building himself a home, finding a wife, and enjoying life. Bumpkin does not believe that there are any thieves on earth, and so he is easily befriended by the two Wangs. They are just about to relieve him of his money when they change their minds and decide to protect him instead: he is so naive and so appealing that they are moved by his simple goodness. They therefore live up to his illusion that there are no thieves on earth.

Jack Ma felt that the role of this Bumpkin was tailor-made for promoting Alipay. He invested some $1.2 million (RMB 10 million) on a promotion campaign that linked the show's celebrities with Alipay: ads connecting the two in people's minds were everywhere. Taobao's symbol was well placed in the TV show; later every prop used by actors in the show was sold at auction on Taobao. There were spin-off products from the show, and other forms of partnering between its producers and Alibaba. Ma then invited the Huayi brothers, giants in the Chinese film world, to film an ad specifically for Alipay. They brought together a number of the original actors and actresses. In the ad, however, Bumpkin is not really foolish; on the contrary, he cleverly goes through the new payment method called Alipay to transfer his money. He also avoids having to pay the large remittance fee that he might normally have had to pay at a bank, an amount with which he "could have bought a mule." The message came across as "With Alipay, there can be no thieves on earth," and the security and basic concepts of Alipay were driven home.

Casting Off the Old Self Without Changing the Bones

Alipay helped launch Taobao and make it a success, but Alipay was never considered merely an accessory to that company, according to Taobao's COO, Sun Danyu. "Alipay came out in October 2003, and thinking back on it now we realize that China's e-commerce market would be nothing like as mature as it has become with that payment intermediary." A senior executive of Alipay confirms that Jack Ma's intention in launching Alipay was not to serve Taobao, but to benefit the entire e-commerce industry. "He wanted to resolve the payment problem of the whole domestic Internet business, not merely to give Taobao a way to resolve its payment problems. As a result, Alipay had to separate out from Taobao, become an independent entity and a genuine third-party platform."

Alipay split off from Taobao in the spring of 2005. Jack Ma had just returned from Davos, Switzerland, where he attended the World Economic Forum, held there every year. As a proselytizer for China's e-commerce, he had given a speech called "2005, the Year of Secure E-Commerce Payment in China." The idea of making Alipay an independent entity was implemented shortly afterward: the intent was to make it the online payment standard for the entire Chinese e-commerce industry. Ma recognized that for Alipay to become the gold standard, it had to differentiate itself and separate itself financially from Alibaba and Taobao. Otherwise, companies such as eBay-EachNet would be threatened by it and not use it. If, on the other hand, Alipay could become a generally used platform in the industry, the benefits that would bring to Alibaba in terms of business revenue would be huge.

The Taobao Web site was launched in May 2003. On July 7, 2003, Alibaba announced that Taobao had been spun off as a separate and independently invested C2C Web site. Alipay was put into use in October 2003. Now, after slightly more than one year, it too was spun off as a separate entity. Transactions on both Alibaba and Taobao were encouraged to use Alipay as their payment platform. One incentive was the slogan "complete compensation," which meant that if anyone bought anything on Alibaba and paid through Alipay and later found that he had been cheated, Alibaba would make complete compensation for the loss. "We're not just talking about a few hundred or a few thousand," clarified Jack Ma. "If the loss is one hundred million, we'll pay." Transactions for large sums did indeed start going through Alipay as confidence in the system increased. One buyer in Shanghai used Alipay to purchase $62,500 (RMB 500,000) worth of pearls; another in Xiamen bought a Buick sedan worth $37,500 (RMB 300,000) through Alipay.

Even as Alipay was aiming to be the technical standard inside China for payment, eBay-EachNet was developing its own product and intending to launch it soon. The news that eBay-EachNet was investing $100 million in its China company got attention: everyone wondered what this amount of money was going to be spent on. As rumors went around, the COO of eBay-EachNet, Zheng Xigui, announced that it would be used to strengthen the security of Internet transactions and especially to provide secure payment methods. At the same time, Zheng revealed that the company would be setting up a call center in order to improve the customer experience.

There was a strong smell of gunpowder in eBay's China policy, meaning that the company was not merely rattling sabers but was setting off the big guns. Unfortunately for eBay, the regulatory environment in China is not conducive to international companies entering the e-commerce payment system. PayPal, eBay's previous platform, ran up against domestic policy restrictions and was initially unable to enter China successfully, but eBay did not stop trying. It invited people with strong expertise in

Internet payment in China's banking circles to join its alliance. It hinted that setting up an independent China-run company was not an impossibility; the resulting platform, called An-Fu-Bao, is very like a Chinese edition of PayPal. At present, PayPal is the global leader in e-commerce transactions. Its information accounts have replaced checks and credit cards as the main means of e-commerce accounting and payment. For a relatively low procedural fee, users can execute payment quickly; PayPal holds 90 percent of the American market and is considered to be dominant internationally as well.

Other competitors eyed the market in China, for the simple reason that astonishingly large profits can be made. Faced with these contenders, and with the deep pockets of eBay-EachNet, Jack Ma decided to play his trump card. Again, it was called "free." Unlike other Web sites, both buyer and seller could use Alipay for their transaction without paying any fee. Most e-commerce sites take a fee for each transaction; Alibaba and Taobao use a different business model that relies on value-added services for which they charge a fee. As a result, they can make a transaction "transparent," allowing buyer and seller to talk to one another without fear of losing control over the deal. Most sites do not allow this: only when the transaction is done can buyer and seller communicate directly. This strategy helped Jack Ma in his competition with the Chinese equivalent of PayPal. Another thing that contributed to Alipay's success has been PayPal's excessive reliance on credit cards. This has meant the company is stymied in China, where credit card use is not as widespread. Turning the situation around to widespread use of credit cards in China is going to take some time.

On February 2, 2005, Jack Ma announced an "elevation in grade" of the online payment tool Alipay. Whether in the same city or in other regions of the country, going through Alipay for a transaction would not incur fees. Ma said that through strategic cooperative relations with Chinese banks, including the Industrial and Commercial Bank of China (ICBC), Construction Bank, Agricultural Bank, and Merchants Bank, Alipay was extending its service to support enterprise users on Alibaba. Any users could voluntarily register to obtain an Alipay account and thus go through this credit intermediary to carry out free funds transfers.

Trade accomplished through Alipay exploded after this announcement. Cooperating with Alipay incurred costs for the banks, but Ma announced that Alibaba would be absorbing these for the time being. He had committed to three years of free service to Taobao users, "and so these intermediary fees naturally have to be borne by us." This was an almost necessary concession.

In July 2005, news hit China that PayPal had officially landed in China and established strategic partnerships with a banking consortium. As China faced the prospect of increased competition within its borders with full entry into the WTO, many different industries began to form groups for self-defense, various forms of alliances and partnerships. In Chinese parlance, such alliances were given a martial arts spin and called *wu lin* alliances, after the forest (*lin*) in which martial arts were practiced. The purpose of such alliances is to create an effective barrier to entry for foreign competitors. Chinese government regulations have served to buttress certain industries that are exempt from full WTO compliance due to national security considerations: these include the Internet, banking, media, and publishing. As head of Alibaba, Jack Ma is considered to be "chief among the *wu lin* masters." He is now contending with very significant forces, however, since the Hong Kong tycoon Li Ka-shing has joined up with eBay in its assault on the China market.

Which system will become the gold standard in payment platforms in China? Ma's answer to this is perhaps most telling:

"Any standard has to be decided by the market. Only when customers really feel you are best will you win their support. Then you get bigger, and then you become the standard. It is a very natural process." The fact that eBay has now linked up with TOM Group, an insider in China business with greater latitude in the regulatory environment, will unavoidably present Alibaba with challenging duels in the future. At present, Alipay remains in the lead in China, supported by such Web sites as Sohu, Baidu, Jiangmin, Jinshan, and others. The sparring of the two contenders continues, however, and as Jack Ma says, only time and the market will prove who wins in the end.

chapter 7

How Can You Catch a Tiger if You Don't Go into His Lair?

The word for "tiger" in Chinese is pronounced *hoo*. The founders of Yahoo! may not have thought of this when they chose the company name, but everyone in China thinks of Yahoo! as a tiger. Jack Ma was particularly fond of this allusion when it came to bearding the Yahoo! lion (in this case tiger) in his lair. In August 2005, Alibaba and Yahoo! China set up a strategic cooperation valued at $1 billion that involved the transfer of all of Yahoo! China's assets to Alibaba and the transfer of 40 percent of Alibaba shares to Yahoo!

In early February 2008, Microsoft put in a hostile takeover bid to buy the global Yahoo! The amount Microsoft offered was $44.6 billion. Google tried to delay or derail the deal since it would threaten Google's dominance of Internet advertising. Two dragons were indeed competing for a sizable pearl: $40 billion is spent annually on online advertising, and this amount is expected to double in the next two years. How a Microsoft takeover of Yahoo! would affect the business of Yahoo! China and Alibaba is not known, but it would necessarily have ripple effects since Yahoo! owns 39 percent of the Alibaba Group. The offer was opposed by Yahoo! founder Jerry Yang as well as other members of the board, and on July 25, 2008, Microsoft's CEO, Steve Ballmer, announced that Microsoft was no longer in negotiations with Yahoo! but left the door open for future talks. There will almost certainly be further talks, and they will have an impact on Alibaba.

As noted, Yahoo! was founded by Jerry Yang and David Filo in the United States in the mid-1990s. Jerry Yang had come to the States from Taiwan and is known in China by his Chinese name, Yang Zhiyuan. In January 1994, the two men created "Jerry's Guide to the World Wide Web" while studying electrical engineering at Stanford University in California. As graduate students, they were in a privileged position, and some of the initial $1 million funding for their venture came from the university itself. In April the name of the how-to guide was changed to Yahoo! and the extraordinary story of this innovative company began. It had started as a way to link information sources that the two men most enjoyed. When the Web sites they collected became too numerous, they began to categorize them into types, and they set up a number of menus, or contents, for ease of use. Originally a system for their own use, the categorization turned out to be beneficial for others. Yahoo! was listed on the Nasdaq exchange in 1996 and moved quickly into Japan, where it met with initial success. The dot-com crisis of 2000 and 2001 took the shares to an all-time low, but the company pulled out of the slump and continued to expand through strategic acquisitions. In March 2004 Yahoo! launched its own search engine technology. In 2005 it celebrated its tenth anniversary, and on August 11 of that year it completed a cross-ownership alliance with Alibaba. com in China.

By 2007 Yahoo!'s revenues worldwide exceeded $6.7 billion, and employees totaled over 11,400. Co-founder Jerry Yang replaced former CEO Terry Semel as head of the company in June 2007, however. Semel had been hired to help turn around the flagging company, but his stewardship was not enough to raise the stock. Earnings continued to decline when Jerry Yang retook the helm.

Yahoo! in China

Inside China, as the head of the combined local forces of Yahoo! and Alibaba, Jack Ma was widely regarded not only as the head of a colossus but as a courageous man for daring to hold on to a tiger. This tiger was known to be lean and hungry in China. It had spent seven years learning the ropes in a very difficult environment. Although it was one of the earliest portals in the United States, Yahoo!'s experience in China began only in 1999. A man named Zhang Pinghe was president of the China entity at the time, and he recalls the times as exciting and challenging. Yahoo! enjoyed a clear first-to-market advantage in China; the three large Chinese portals at the time, Sina, Sohu, and NetEase, had already burned through most of their money. Yahoo! in China soon encountered funding problems: not only was financial support from headquarters small but the company was ordered to turn a profit as soon as possible. This was in line with Jerry Yang's philosophy: in the United States, the company became profitable within its first ten months. In China, however, the model was hard to duplicate, and the company began to struggle. Yahoo! was not suited to the local conditions, and because of that it found itself in awkward circumstances. Its name recognition was much lower than that of the three main portals, and Yahoo!'s search engine functions could not compete either with the locally developed Baidu or with Google. In the instant-messaging market, it lost out to QQ and MSN. In the online auction market, it found itself outmaneuvered by eBay's child in China, EachNet.

By early 2001 Zhang Pinghe had left the company, disillusioned. For the next several years a succession of professional managers were brought in from outside China to try to turn the company around. Low morale set in, the decision-making process back at headquarters was too slow, and it was generally acknowledged that Yahoo! in China was not working out.

At the end of 2003, Jerry Yang found a person inside China who understood search engines and who was eager to test himself at Yahoo! This was a man named Zhou Hongwei, who had been leading his own team in China, known as 3721. Zhou brought his entire team at 3721 over to Yahoo! China. Although he only led the company for the next two years, he was able to achieve some success. Frustrated that market share did not rise, Zhou posed a key question to Jerry Yang: "Do you want to grow the company, or do you need to see immediate profit?" After thinking it over for six months, Yang decided that the primary goal should be growth, not profit. Unfortunately, the decision came too late for some. Zhou left the company, ten senior engineers jumped over to Baidu and other search engine companies, and a number of other employees left over the next five months. By the time Alibaba began expressing an interest in strategic cooperation, morale inside Yahoo! China was at an all-time low.

Jerry Yang's enthusiasm for the China market never wavered.

He had put tremendous investment into the effort, including the early hiring of IT industry managers, the huge amount paid for 3721, and the costs of localization, however inadequate that was. Nothing had allowed the company to live up to its reputation for being a real tiger. In the end, Yang adopted the strategy of total localization: he decided to transfer assets to Alibaba, at the same time preserving the Yahoo! brand. He allowed Alibaba complete operating control in developing Yahoo! China.

A Chinese proverb relates how to catch a monkey: you put something very sweet in a cage and let the monkey put his hand through the bars to try to get it. Once the monkey has the sweetness in its grasp, it tries to pull the prize out but finds that its clenched fist can't squeeze back through the bars. The monkey has caught himself—its own fist prevents it from being free. The only way the monkey can save itself is by letting go, opening its hand and releasing what is holding it back. Jerry Yang was intelligent enough to "open his hand," thereby saving himself: he released Yahoo! in China, entrusting Jack Ma to "keep the tiger" and to make sure it lived.

The cause of Yahoo! China's seven-year itch—its malaise for that long stretch of time—was, in general, indecision. According to previous managers, the company couldn't make up its mind: it vacillated between this and that, both worried about getting and worried about losing. These unfortunate years allowed Jerry Yang to reconsider the future direction of the company and to countenance the idea of its developing under a new identity.

It is said that Jerry Yang and Jack Ma came together for a golf meeting in the United States to discuss possibilities on May 1, 2005. Then, on August 6, Baidu listed on the market and a whole series of actions by Google raised the ante. This sparked both men into action. Jerry Yang telephoned Ma and suggested a price. Ma came back with a proposal: $1 billion for 40 percent of shares but only 35 percent of voting rights. The deal was quickly made and announced to the public on August 11. "I like to look forward," Jerry Yang commented as the deal became known in the news. "No matter whether it is decisions about the market or the company, Yahoo! hasn't made any major mistakes." Yang feels that starting a company is akin to a spurt of adrenaline, whereas running a company and growing a company is a marathon. His goal was to create a long-standing company and his investment in China was strategic: his plan for China had never changed. He sent an e-mail message to all Yahoo! China employees that said, "This morning we have announced the formation of a strategic cooperation with Alibaba. . . . This is an exciting moment for Yahoo! people, and I hope that you will recognize the enormous opportunity ahead and become a member of this successful team."

Who Bought Whom?

When the long-rumored merger or "strategic cooperation" between the two companies received public confirmation, the ongoing question of who had bought whom did not receive much clarification. Alibaba acquired all of Yahoo! China's assets and at the same time received $1 billion from Yahoo! in investment in order to create China's most powerful Internet search platform. Alibaba and Yahoo! made simultaneous announcements in China, the United States, and Japan. This was the largest merger to date in the history of China's Internet.

Jack Ma joked that Alibaba and Yahoo! had sweet-talked each other for seven years, and that on China's equivalent of Valentine's Day (August 11), they were getting married. More seriously, he noted that the new team intended to create the strongest Internet search platform in China and to remain a Chinese enterprise with global influence. The assets that Alibaba acquired include

Yahoo!'s portal in China, its search technology, its information and advertising businesses, and its authentication and verification service. Alibaba also received exclusive user rights within China to the Yahoo! brand for an unlimited period. At the same time, Yahoo! became Alibaba's largest strategic investor, with 40 percent of economic benefits (shares) and 35 percent of voting rights. Ma steadfastly declared to the outside world that this was a purchase of Yahoo! China by Alibaba, but the press was not convinced it was so. Many could not help but wonder who was in fact buying whom. In the face of all kinds of rumors, it would probably be hard to know for some time.

Ma declared that he was "working every day at Yahoo! China," but when he received members of the press, he did it only in his own offices at Alibaba, which indicated a sensitivity about image. As for doubts in the industry about whether Yahoo! had really invested $1 billion, Ma parried the thrusts of journalists. "All financial details with regard to the acquisition will be announced within eighteen months," he said. "At that time, you can make up your own minds." As to what he might be intending to do with $1 billion, Ma noted, "It's pretty hard to digest a huge amount of money. When you've just swallowed down something enormous, it is a challenge for your stomach. One billion may look good to people on the outside, but it is undeniably a huge challenge to us."

More precise information came with the SEC Form 8-K, filed August 16, 2005. The transaction was described as a "strategic combination." It involved many more transactions than just the principal one. These included purchase of Taobao shares from Softbank ($360 million, paid for by Yahoo!). They involved purchase of Alibaba shares from certain Alibaba shareholders for an aggregate figure of $570 million. After all the transactions, the result was that Yahoo! owned approximately 40 percent of outstanding shares of Alibaba on a fully diluted basis, including shares reserved for issuance under Alibaba's employee stock plans and upon exercise of outstanding options, warrants, and the convertible bond issued to Softbank. Alibaba, for its part, then owned 100 percent of the outstanding shares of Taobao.

Ma's official statement about the transaction was upbeat: "Teaming up with Yahoo! will allow us to deliver an unmatched range of e-commerce services to businesses and consumers in China. With the addition of Yahoo! China to Alibaba.com's business, we are expanding our services to provide a leading search offering to China's Internet users. Alibaba.com is winning in B2B in China, winning in C2C, winning in online payments, and now we're going to win in search."

Masayoshi Son also had some comments, since his Softbank was a crucial party to the deal. He disagreed with some opinions that the $4 billion valuation of the new company was too high. "I think it's too low," he said. "That's why we are not selling our entire stake. It's a signal of our confidence that this company will grow much more." It was generally felt that the newly combined forces of Alibaba and Yahoo! in China were a serious threat to eBay. Yahoo! had beat out eBay in Japan as well as Taiwan. A combined Taobao and Yahoo! were now on the warpath to beat eBay in China.

Who Runs the Show?

In the face of questions from reporters, Jack Ma was clear on the subject of who was boss. Journalists wondered how he was going to manage what might be a sticky relationship with Yahoo! headquarters in the States. Ma did not mince words. "Many people are asking what the reporting relationship is going to be with America. I tell them that in China Jerry Yang should report to me. I am chairman of the board. He is a board member. I am his boss, he is not my boss. All of the decision making is right here in China."

This was in line with Ma's conviction that Alibaba had to be a China-born and China-run company. Political considerations inside China's regulatory structure dictate a high degree of "native son" identity. At the same time, Ma was playing for bigger stakes than just China. He recognized that China's economy and demographics meant that it was inevitable that country would be in the forefront of global e-commerce in the near future. Playing for global stakes meant that a China base was an asset, not, as many had previously assumed, a liability. Meanwhile, new employees from Yahoo! China had to be inducted into the peculiarly positive way of thinking of Alibaba's chairman. Jack Ma gave them their first lesson in a speech made to employees. He titled the speech "Edison Tricked the World." The original manuscript has been lost, but an employee who was present when Ma delivered it reconstructed the gist of the text:

> Today is the first time I am meeting with our new Yahoo! friends in person. I want to thank you for coming. I also want to share with you some reasons for success, even though most of you will probably not benefit from them. Since you are all hardworking and intelligent, you will probably reject my comments out of hand. A few of you may be lazy enough to get something out of them, however. Let's get to the point. There are many extremely clever people in the world. And there are lots of well-educated people who seem unable to succeed. This is because they've been wrongly taught from an early age. They have developed the habit of being overly diligent and hardworking. Many of these people remember Edison's famous phrase, the one about genius being 99 percent sweat and the rest inspiration. They have been led around by the nose by this saying for their entire lives. I'm telling you now it's

wrong. If you plod forward with diligence, in the end you'll be left with nothing. Edison was in fact too lazy to consider the real reasons for his success—that is why he came out with that phrase and tricked the whole world. It's time for us to rethink the facts. Some of you may think I am talking nonsense. Let me give you one hundred examples that prove you are wrong. Facts, after all, trump any argument. The richest man on earth, Bill Gates, was a programmer who was too lazy to study at school, so he dropped out. He was also too lazy to remember all those complex DOS commands, so he built that graphic interface ... what was it called? I've forgotten. I'm too lazy to remember these things. The result was that the entire world now uses that "face," that "window," and he has become the world's richest man.

Then there is the most valuable brand on earth, Coca-Cola. The boss of Coca-Cola was even more lazy. China's tea culture has a long and venerable history, Brazil's coffee is delicious, but this guy was too lazy to go looking for them. He put a little sugar together with some water, packaged it in a bottle and sold it, and called it Coca-Cola. The rest is history. The entire world is drinking this liquid that looks a little like blood. Then soccer. The best soccer player in the world is [Ronaldo], who is fundamentally too lazy to move around much on the field. He just stands before the goal of the other side. He waits for the ball to come near him, then gives it a kick. As one of the highest-paid athletes in the world, people puff him up and say he runs with the ball faster than anyone. It's not true. Other people run for ninety minutes; he runs for fifteen seconds. Naturally he is considered faster.

Fast food. The most successful fast-food company in the world is McDonald's. Its boss was lazy in the extreme: too lazy to study the refinements of French cooking or the complex skill of Chinese cuisine. He just stuck a piece of beef in between two chunks of bread and as a result the world has this *M* sign all over it. The pizza boss is the same. We Chinese have *lao bing* [a kind of stuffed flat bread], with all the things inside. This man was too lazy to stick anything inside; he puts it right on top and sells it as pizza. It's the same materials but his pizza costs ten times as much as *lao bing*.

Then there are other, more clever lazy people. They were too lazy to climb stairs, so they invented elevators. They were too lazy to walk, so they invented cars, trains, airplanes. They were too lazy to kill people one by one, so they invented nuclear bombs. They were too lazy to work out every calculation, so they invented mathematical formulas. Too many examples. I'm too lazy to give any more.

Oh yes, and then there is that other bit of nonsense I want to mention, about how you have to be in frantic motion in order to stay healthy. How many athletes do you see growing old? Not so many. The longest-lived people on earth are those monks who sit around and are too lazy to eat meat!

What would our lives be like right now without all these lazy people? I'm too lazy to think about it. People are like this, but animals too. The tortoise, said to be the longest-living animal on earth—well, tortoises hardly move at all. They just crouch there and as a result live to be a thousand. But compared to rabbits, who are diligent, and who run around all the time . . . who wins? Cows are the most diligent, and as a result people give them nothing but grass to eat and then add the insult of squeezing them for milk. Pandas, in contrast, are lazy things that do nothing at all. They just sit there gnawing on a piece of bamboo all day. What do people do with them? They protect them and call them "national treasures"!

To return to our work: You see people running around here in the company. Are they the ones who are most highly paid? Absolutely not. Those most highly paid sit around looking carefree. They probably have a lot of stock options as well. The examples I give are just to clarify an issue, which is that, in fact, this world relies on lazy people to carry it forward. The world is marvelous, thanks to them. Now you should all be aware of the reason for your lack of success!

Laziness is not, of course, stupid-lazy. If you want to be able to work less, you have to think of ways to do it, clever ways to be allowed to be lazy. You have to have a lazy style, a lazy state of mind. Like me. I've been lazy since I was a child. Look how short I am—I was even too lazy to grow. That's the state of mind you need to cultivate.

Thank you all again!

Yahoo! China Challenges Google and Baidu

Search engines are big business: it is estimated that by 2009 the value of the advertising market on search engines in America alone will grow to over $5 billion. China's market is smaller but is expected to come near $1 billion by 2010. All of the globe's major players are picking up the pace in China in order to occupy that vital part of the Internet market.

The major search engine players in China are Baidu and Google. Over the course of 2004 and 2005, these two surged ahead of competitors, most importantly ahead of Yahoo! China. Baidu's 33.1 percent of the market in 2004 rose to 46.5 percent in 2005. Google's 22.4 percent of the market rose to 26.9 percent in 2005. Yahoo! China, meanwhile, lost ground. Its market share went from 30.2 percent to 15.6 percent. After Alibaba acquired Yahoo! China, Jack Ma decided to implement a total revision of the Yahoo! site, and he did it to resemble the Google look.

Google is the greatest competitor for the search engine market in the world. Google not only maintains a firm hold on the Western market but since 2005 has systematically begun a campaign in China. China's own local company, Baidu, was listed on Nasdaq at the end of 2005, and the extravagant rise in its price swiftly turned all eyes in its direction. All of this was difficult for Jerry Yang to accept, understanding as he did the importance of the China market. Most people believe that the reason he was willing to relinquish Yahoo! China to Alibaba was not merely that Yahoo! China was in difficult straits but more importantly that competitive global pressure was forcing him to undertake a by-pass strategy. Yahoo!'s cooperation with Alibaba has always had the shadow of Google behind it. Once Microsoft started bidding for Yahoo! the struggle for the pearl between the two mightiest dragons in the world was on. Since the contest started, Microsoft and Yahoo! have engaged in on-again, off-again negotiations that, as of this writing, are on hold.

If Yahoo! fell behind in the China market, it clearly would have no chance in the future to overtake Google on the wider stage, and Ma was aware of the odds. In the second half of 2005, he mobilized a transformation campaign at Yahoo! China. He began with the simple slogan, "In China, Yahoo! is search, and search is Yahoo!" He publicly declared that Yahoo! fully intended to sit at the place of honor in China's search engine market. In order to achieve this transformation, Ma did three things. First, he threw out the homepage of the previous Yahoo! China site, replacing it with a starkly simple page that initiated searches. This homage to Google's homepage made it clear that, indeed, search was Yahoo! and Yahoo! was search. Second, he forecast a wildly optimistic figure for Yahoo! China's revenues in 2006. The figure was so outrageous that few took it seriously: everyone felt that Jack Ma was under great pressure and that he often used the device of self-encouragement to whip up enthusiasm and spur performance. Ma was, after all, a teacher and knew how to draw out the potential in students. Third, he clarified what Alibaba meant by "search" and how that fit into the overall strategy of the parent company.

In doing this, it became apparent that his search goals for Yahoo! China and the search goals of Google were different.

Ma's overarching strategy for the company maintains a clear focus on the business of e-commerce. "In the coming five years, we will be integrating search in our development of e-commerce," Ma has repeatedly stated. E-commerce remains the holy grail—value-added services for small and medium-sized enterprises remain the driving business model. In explaining this, Ma again uses the analogy of *weiqi* (Go), the Asian game that uses small black and white stones on a grid-lined board. Despite its simple rules, the game requires considerable mental attention. The objective is to gain control of the board by surrounding your opponent's pieces and taking them out of the action. Keeping your own pieces close together reduces their chances of being attacked; keeping your pieces more widely deployed increases your own chances for controlling the board. These two postures are generally conflicting; the player constantly has to consider the balance between defense and offense. Ma enjoys discussing *weiqi* with his favorite author, Louis Cha. It forms his mental landscape when he is thinking about the future of the company. Most people aim for an end result; Ma sees the probabilities in various shifting moves along the way and knows that as the board changes, strategy also shifts. "Those who excel at *weiqi* look at the overall structure," he has said. "Those who are bad at it think just about the final result."

Part of the shifting nature of the "board" in the Internet realm is the way in which technology is gradually being tamed, as it were, and made to suit the needs of human beings. "Right now, search engines are technology-driven; 'search' is a game for engineers," Ma has noted to employees. "It doesn't really take into account the true needs of users. Search should just be a tool. It can't change our lives, whereas the Internet can and will change China."

Ma acquired Yahoo! China because he felt that Alibaba lacked search capability in growing the e-commerce business, and this lack was obstructing growth. After buying Yahoo! China, Ma began to mold the search capabilities in service of Alibaba goals. The general manager for search operations of Yahoo! agrees with that approach: "If you talk in terms of user satisfaction," Tian Jiang declared to an audience at the March 2006 conference on search engine strategies, held in Nanjing, "no matter whether it is Yahoo!'s search functions, or Baidu, or Google, all of them are inadequate. They are the product of engineers' brains; their man-made categorization is not in line with what people need. Technology should be in the service of people, not the other way around. If people are in the service of technology, we have technology for technology's sake. That's just going to frighten users away."

Some have taken exception to this view. Zhou Shaoning, president of Google's Greater China Sales and Business Development Group, is one of them. Zhou's response to Tian Jiang's comments was that de facto change has to be propelled by technology first. The average man in the street cannot dream up the direction and degree of technological change. Only after a product has made an appearance can it be worked upon, modified, adapted. Search in general was a technology that still relied mainly on the input of technicians. At Google, therefore, engineers enjoy the highest positions. "They can deliver. Whatever you ask them to do, they can do," he said proudly. At the same time, he admitted that products created purely by engineers were not necessarily market-ready; they needed the validation of users. Zhou Shaoning has pointed out that the growth of the Internet is creating a tremendous increase in the volume of information. Search is an important method of both gathering and consolidating information. It can raise the efficiency of people's activities and therefore is radically changing people's lives.

At the end of the day, Alibaba and Google have different concepts in mind when they discuss search. They therefore also have different formulations of market strategy. It will be interesting to watch how the different perspectives affect the development of China's future Internet industry.

Search Engines and Keyword Services

"It can work only if it is local." Jack Ma applies this mantra to Internet practices not only in China but also in the United States. "American Yahoo! is based on the needs of America; Alibaba Yahoo! similarly has to be based on the needs of China. It cannot simply copy."

Ma's emphasis was necessary when Yahoo! China came under the Alibaba rubric, for the temptation was to copy and paste the old system into the new. In order to meet the needs not only of the Chinese public but also of the special user groups operating in the realm of Taobao and Alibaba, Ma transformed the old Yahoo! search engine into one that took advantage of paying customers in China. Both Taobao and Alibaba offer paid services that allow clients to put their keywords at the head of search results. This service is connected to the primary rationale of the enterprise, which is to provide useful tools to companies engaged in e-commerce that help them make money. The keyword service is not only an ideal sales tool for Alibaba but also is necessary for enterprises that are using the Internet for their promotion. When buyers search the Alibaba site and come across enterprises in which they may be interested, they can peruse information that includes keyword searches.

Creating a seamless search engine required extremely competent engineers who understood the goals of the overall system.

More importantly, it required an understanding of how to use the integrative capabilities of Internet resources in order to attain the goals of e-commerce. Ma was intentionally creating an e-commerce service with limitless capability. This took advantage of all the various parts of the puzzle that he was drawing together: Alipay, Yahoo!'s search engine, and so on. Ma was bringing seemingly disparate groups into the same arena. By integrating these, he was allowing "no change" to influence "all change," a profoundly misunderstood tenet in Chinese philosophy.

Yahoo! China's share of the China search market had dropped from 30.2 percent to 15.6 percent between 2004 and 2005, and so Jack Ma decided to undertake a total face-lift of the site. In November 2005 he announced to the public that Yahoo! China had changed its format. The homepage had been simplified, as noted earlier. Nonetheless, only three months later, Ma had changed his mind. After returning from a trip to the States, he declared, "When Yahoo! doesn't act like Yahoo! is when it will be really successful." He had just been to visit the forty engineers at the American Yahoo! headquarters who had been merged into Alibaba. He complained to them that they lacked a feel for what the customer needed; they were behaving like, well, engineers. From now on, he hoped that engineers would look at problems from the perspective of users of the Internet. One person later revealed that, as a result, Yahoo! China's homepage would have not only a search box but also under that some hot topics and, under the hot topics, hot content.

In addition to these face-lift changes, Ma began to reorganize Yahoo!'s personnel. He began by pulling together a new high-level management team. He made Tian Jiang, Yahoo! China's general manager, directly responsible to him. Under Tian Jiang came Li Rui, in charge of Yahoo!'s e-mail business as well as deputy general manager of all China business. Directly under him was Mao Xin, in charge of the new search portal business, including the original Yahoo! team. This direct line of command allowed clear communications, in theory, and was helpful in increasing control over any problems that might arise in the course of Yahoo! China's growth. The direct line of command also increased pressure on subordinates. "Ma put a considerable amount of pressure on me," said Tian Jiang. "He demanded that Yahoo! China's page browsing rate be increased by a minimum of 200 percent." In addition, a number of new employees were hired in order to improve the portal. Prior to the merger, Yahoo!'s content department totaled around forty people. Alibaba now increased this, since Ma felt that existing content was too lifeless. He felt that Yahoo! China needed to concentrate its focus on three areas: entertainment, sports, and finance. These three promised the highest number of hits, and entertainment was the area on which Jack Ma chose to focus.

"From now on, Yahoo! will be entering the entertainment field," announced Jack Ma in the early part of the Year of the Dog (2006). Entertainment had been shown to be the one thing most wanted by "Net people." Since Yahoo! Search intended to become China's premier search engine, it followed that Yahoo! had to go into that territory. In January 2006, Jack Ma announced that he was teaming up with Hunan Satellite and the Huayi brothers to develop a completely new form of entertainment show, called *Yahoo! Searches for the Stars*. Through entertainment, *Yahoo! Searches for the Stars* hoped to achieve a daily increase in the numbers of search users. The China Internet Association had predicted that the total search market in China would continue to maintain an annual growth rate of 70 percent over the next three years, as it had in the years just past. The opportunities were considerable.

Jack Ma's January 2006 announcement about moving into entertainment led to a liaison between Yahoo! and three of the most famous movie directors in China: Chen Kaige, Feng Xiaogang, and Zhang Jizhong. In Beijing, Yahoo! Search announced that it was investing $3.75 million (RMB 30 million) in this venture. Each director was invited to make a short ad relating to the subject of Yahoo! Search. The result was to be less of an ad than a short movie, a brief video on the Internet that experimented with the possibilities of the media. Ma addressed the subject in concrete terms. "The content of most interest to the common man on the Internet is entertainment. If Yahoo! Search is to become the premier choice, then it must throw itself wholeheartedly into entertainment, it must lead in entertainment." People in the industry felt that this was a weak spot at that time. Baidu had been strong in entertainment when MP3 searches came in vogue, but it then ran up against copyright infringement of downloaded material and found it necessary to think of a better way to get traffic. Jack Ma felt that short movies or video clips would perhaps be the trend in the near future, and would in any event be able to deliver good promotion results. Chen Kaige, Feng Xiaogang, and Zhang Jizhong were therefore engaged to help deliver the content. The fame of these three men is stupendous in China. Their association with the project was a huge draw for hopeful young men and women of talent.

The general plan in the *Yahoo! Searches for the Stars* was to put out a call for acting and directing talent, somewhat like the initial stages of *American Idol*. Any young person could participate in the contest. From January 4 to late February 2006, judges—including the three directors—would be selecting an initial 150 people to go on to the second stage of the contest. From these, they would choose thirty-six, and then nine, and the final three. These finalists would be Yahoo!'s Stars. The prize: to work together with the three directors in the filming of three short films, as actors or as assistant directors themselves, involved in all stages of the creative process. The plan called for all activities to be broadcast via the Internet, live, in real time. Not only were winners able to work with famous directors, but after the shoot they could, if they wanted, become contracted actors with the Huayi brothers. This was ir-resistible to anyone with dreams of being a star.

Led by the directors, the voters for the event would be the great mass of public Internet users. Voting could be done on the Internet, using something called a Yahoo! Pass. Each holder of a Yahoo! Pass ID was allowed to cast ten votes a day. We will not follow the course of this contest any farther—suffice it to say it was an ingenious way to encourage more traffic on Yahoo!

How Can You See the Rainbow
if You Don't Go Out in the Rain?

Nobody goes out in the rain without getting a little bit wet. As Bill Gates always says of Microsoft, "We expect to get sued. That's just part of the business." Alibaba found the same thing to be true, and it has handled its legal issues with a fair degree of success.

One of the first lawsuits came in 2001 with regard to Alibaba's domain name. In the Alibaba legend, when a person incants the magic words "open sesame," he opens up a treasure trove. In the real world of the Internet, however, the magic words opened up a lawsuit. The plaintiff was the Beijing Zheng Pu Science & Technology Development Company, Ltd, which used the domain name 2688.com. In Chinese, the numbers 2688 are pronounced *erliubaba,* which sounds similar to "Alibaba." This company brought suit against Alibaba for infringing its trademark rights in the Beijing Municipal People's Intermediate Court. The suit was filed on February 1, 2001.

On December 10 of the same year, the court rejected the case and confirmed that Alibaba's Chinese domain should remain lawfully under the registered ownership of Alibaba (China) Internet Technology Company, Ltd. Beijing Zheng Pu did not accept this decision and on December 20 formally appealed to the Municipal Supreme Court. Yao Zengqi, chairman of the board of Zheng Pu, declared, "The court's judgment was groundless, a contradiction from start to end. We can't figure out what the law is supposed to be protecting if it arrives at judgments like this." The vice president of Alibaba (China) in charge of the case, Jin Jianhang, stood his ground. "We will actively fight the appeal, and we will guard the interests of our company and our many users. We can't allow the brand of Alibaba to have any negative influence."

Yao Zengqi disagreed. As he saw it, the company Alibaba had not yet been established when his company registered its trademark. How could he have intended to "snatch" the name of a company that was not yet in existence? Alibaba refuted this with the statement that it had begun using the names on both Chinese and English Web sites that Jack Ma started unofficially at the end of 1998 and officially launched in March 1999. Zheng Pu registered the domain name 2688.com four months after the name Alibaba had come into regular use. Zheng Pu was clearly aiming at Alibaba in registering this name—and the Beijing courts refused to legitimize the subterfuge.

Following is the official text associated with this case. This should put to rest any doubts that the Chinese government is serious about enforcing an international code with respect to Internet intellectual property rights:

> In November 2000, the China Internet Network Information Center ("CNNIC"), which manages China's top-level domain name with the suffix ".cn" and their Chinese equivalents, granted the Chinese "ALIBABA" domain name to Alibaba. CNNIC had reserved the "ALIBABA" domain name under the principle that it was a famous Internet name that should belong to Alibaba, the company that operates the Web site, www.alibaba.com. CNNIC had implemented this reservation policy for a number of other well-known Internet companies in China including sina.com and sohu.com. However, Alibaba's legal ownership of the name was challenged by Beijing Zheng Pu Technology Development Co., Ltd. ("Zheng Pu"), a Beijing-based software re-seller, who brought the lawsuit against CNNIC and Alibaba in Beijing in February 2001. Zheng Pu claimed that due to CNNIC's reservation policy, it was not able to register the "ALIBABA" domain name in CNNIC's on-line registration system, and it challenged the legality of Alibaba's ownership of the domain name.
>
> In its ruling, the Court pointed out that Zheng Pu had no basis for its claim to the "ALIBABA" domain name because it provided no evidence of any rights to any intellectual property relating to the name. Although Zheng Pu had applied to register "ALIBABA" as its trademark, which application is contested by Alibaba as having been submitted in bad faith with the intent of unfair competition, the Court found that mere submission of a trademark application does not give rise to any legal rights to the name until it is registered. The Court further stated that Alibaba should be the rightful owner of the domain name because Alibaba is the company that created the renowned ALIBABA brand based on the Internet web site www.alibaba.com and the commercial value associated with the brand.

The court also stated: "In the circumstance where the Alibaba Web site is already well known among Internet users, registration of the domain name by someone else could confuse Internet users and be detrimental to the rights of Alibaba, thereby constituting unfair competition." In light of China's entry into the WTO and its commitment to enforce protection of well-known global brand names against unfair competition, the court's opinion sounds consistent with the spirit of fairness in intellectual property protection.

"We applaud the Court's decision," said Alibaba CEO Jack Ma after the verdict was announced. "This landmark case shows that the court recognizes the national and international brand that Alibaba has built up in our business. We are pleased that the Chinese administrative and legal systems are protecting the intellectual property rights of the rightful owners and preventing opportunists from taking advantage of other people's hard work."

Another legal matter, this time initiated by Alibaba, concerned the company Taobao. On April 20, 2004, Taobao's COO declared to the world that the company had absolute proof that Yahoo! China was siphoning large quantities of data from its servers. Taobao raised an official protest against this behavior. COO Sun Danyu said that Taobao had analyzed the problems and, after ruling out internal server problems, realized it was dealing with a very sophisticated hacker. Using high-powered software tools, this hacker was grabbing hold of Taobao's commercial statistics and proprietary data. On further investigation, Taobao discovered that the IP of the hacker was owned by none other than . . . Yahoo! China.

Yahoo! China denied the charge and noted that since it was a Web site with search engine functions, it often took in large amounts of data in the course of automatic searches. The Taobao Incident had arisen in the course of a normal search and had simply caused a large amount of product data and seller information to be downloaded from Taobao to Yahoo! The issue was not unique to Yahoo!: Taobao claimed that eBay-EachNet had also been using "improper competition" to hack into Taobao servers in the past. Such problems were referred to Chinese authorities and eventually resolved by superior competition of the stronger party, whether it was strictly legitimate or not. Meanwhile, in August 2005, Alibaba and Yahoo! China came to their agreement to merge forces.

Yahoo! China: Challenges After the Acquisition

The combining of Alibaba and Yahoo! China forces confronted Jack Ma with several major dilemmas. First and foremost was how to keep to the e-commerce focus when Yahoo! was a portal with a wealth of other capabilities. Second was how to reallocate human resources in a way that did not capsize the boat, and third was how to capitalize on the Yahoo! brand.

Alibaba had single-mindedly focused on e-commerce. With Yahoo! its scope of business now extended to information content, search, and such other Internet service functions as e-mail and instant messaging. Should Alibaba try to turn Yahoo! China into an e-commerce company? Or should Yahoo! China retain its portal functions but undergo "localization"? This question had to be resolved in tandem with the redeployment of human resources. At the first meeting between all Yahoo! China employees and Jack Ma, the former president of Yahoo! China, Zhou Hongwei, unexpectedly showed up and asked to be allowed to speak. He raised only one request in his speech, and that was that Alibaba deal squarely with Yahoo! China employees, finding them positions. This was seen to be somewhat draconian and made the whole process of merging forces even more difficult.

Capitalizing on Yahoo!'s brand name was equally trouble-some. Google and Baidu dominate the search market in China, and it has not been clear whether Yahoo! can overcome such competitors, which have a strong lead in habitual consumer use. Yahoo! is only the fourth largest portal in China, yet it still enjoys a brand name that is the envy of many. Wielding that brand name in the search market has been Ma's primary goal. Daily habits of search consumers are quite established, however, and it is not clear whether Ma will succeed. Despite his efforts to bring technical experts to China who have been meeting one-on-one with Chinese developers in a Herculean effort to develop the platform, there have been many doubters.

Chinese enjoy watching bloody battles between contenders: many find it amusing to see the strong eat the weak in a fight for the survival of the fittest. There is no reason to believe at this stage that Jack Ma will disappoint his audience. He has been known to pull unusual moves in the past, and he doubtless will again in the future.

The stakes in all these lawsuits and competitive postures are increasingly large. The next section describes just how large, according to the most recent (January 2008) research on the Internet in China.

Status of the Internet in China

On January 17, 2008, China's authoritative CNNIC issued its twenty-first annual report on the state of the Internet in China. The first line of this report declares that the total number of "Net people" in China is 210 million, 5 million fewer than in the United States. The numbers have already changed, however, and Chinese users now surpass the number in the United States.

From being a country that forbade mention of the Internet a dozen years ago, China now dominates Internet communications. How this affects the *weiqi* board of Internet players is unclear, but it is certain that any strategic moves by global players must take China into consideration.

Since China is so crucial in global strategies for these companies, the following section gives a summary of CNNIC's evaluation of the Internet in China in 2008. It is a translated and summarized version of the Chinese text available on the Internet.

CNNIC Report Summary

CNNIC forecasts that in the early to middle part of 2008, China will become the country with the greatest number of Internet users in the world. The rate of increase in number of users in China is 16 percent, which is still lower than the average worldwide rate of 19.1 percent.

For the first time, CNNIC has done a detailed analysis of the composition of new Internet users in China in this report. Among new users in 2007, the trends are clear: the increase is fastest among people under the age of eighteen and over the age of thirty. Although the greatest increases are among the young and the educated, the statistics show that more and more lower-income people are now accessing the Internet.

People in farming villages are becoming an important segment of new users. Forty percent of the 73 million new users in 2007 are in towns and villages, which means that 29.17 million new users are rural Chinese. By the end of December 2007, the number of people in China's farming villages that access the Internet had reached 52.62 million with a 127.7 percent annual rate of increase. This statistic indicates that villages in China hold huge potential for becoming Internet market consumers. Various government policies have focused on connecting villages to national communications networks, whether via telephone or cable: the goal of such policies is to "informationize" these communities and broaden their Internet access. Rates of current usage and increasing trends show that the market potential, now being realized in villages, is absolutely vast.

Surveys taken for the report indicate that Internet use has evolved in China and entertainment has become the most important application. The percentages of people who confirm they use the Internet for specific purposes include the following seven categories: music (86.6 percent), instant messaging (81.4 percent), videos (76.9 percent), news (73.6 percent), search engines (72.4 percent), games (59.3 percent), and e-mail (56.5 percent).

In contrast to many parts of the world, much of Internet access in China is via high-speed broadband connections. Over 163 million people now access the Internet via broadband connections in China; 50.4 million people access through handheld devices. Both of these types of access are rapidly increasing.

In terms of geographic distribution, access to the Internet in Beijing and Shanghai is highest, with 46.6 percent of the population of Beijing and 45.8 percent of the population in Shanghai accessing the Internet. The greatest rate of increase, however, is in Guangdong province, due to the influence of handheld devices. Within this past year, usage in that province alone has increased by 15 million people.

At present, 140 million people access the Internet from their homes in China. This is an increase of 35.7 percent over last year. Home access through computer is via 78 million computers, meaning roughly two people access per each home computer. The greatest concentration of access via computer is in Guangdong province, Beijing, and Shanghai. The average cost per home for home access is $10.26 per month (74.9 RMB), or an annual total access fee of $123 (900 RMB) per household; 67.3 percent of all Internet users access the Internet from home. In addition, 33.9 percent of all users access from Internet cafes, and 24.3 percent access from their workplace. The average cost of accessing the Internet from Internet cafes is $7.07 per month (51.6 RMB). Access from home is rising rapidly, while access at the workplace is level with only a slight increase.

At present, China has 50.4 million people accessing the Internet via handheld devices. Around two-thirds (66.5 percent) of all those accessing via handheld devices are male, and most of these are between the ages of eighteen and twenty-four. Some 94 percent of people who access the Internet use desktop computers; 26.7 percent use laptops, and 24.0 percent use handheld devices. Clearly there is overlap among these three user groups, with some accessing in more than one way.

Of people with a high school education in China, 83.35 million have not yet accessed the Internet, while 437 million people who have a middle-school education have not yet accessed the Internet. The most important reasons given are that these people do not understand computers or the Internet itself, they do not have time, and they do not have the equipment.

To those who do access the Internet, the practice has become a necessary function in daily life. The average length of time spent on the Internet per week, by users overall, is 16.2 hours. People who use the Internet give it high marks in terms of its usefulness to them: 93.1 percent say it is extremely useful to work and study; 38.3 percent say they feel they have missed something if they haven't been on the Internet at least once a day.

In terms of media on the Internet: 73.6 percent of people interviewed have used the Internet to read news in the past half year. The percentage of people finding Internet news "believable" or "true" is 51.3 percent. The entertainment value of the Internet is rated somewhat higher. Use of the Net for gaming totals 59.3 percent among all users; on average an Internet user playing games on the Internet accesses the Internet for 7.3 hours per week for this purpose. Of all Internet users surveyed, 71.2 percent have downloaded music within the past half year, 76.9 percent have watched online videos, and 40.5 percent have downloaded videos.

Purchasing of goods on the Internet is increasing: 22.1 percent of all users have bought goods via the Internet this past year. The higher the level of education, the higher the amount of Web purchases. On average, in the past half year an Internet buyer has purchased $64 (RMB 466) worth of goods on the Internet.

China-based domain names now total 11.93 million, an increase of 190.4 percent over last year. The main increase has come in the use of the domain name .cn, which now totals some 9 million registered sites, a fourfold increase over the number in 2006. There are now 135 million IP addresses in China, an increase of 38 percent over the previous year. At present there are 1,029 IP addresses for every ten thousand people; there are 6,442 IP addresses for every ten thousand Internet users.

There are 1.5 million Web sites in China. Among these, slightly over one million have a .cn domain address and .cn domain names constitute 66.9 percent of all Web sites in China.

As for problems with the Internet, viruses are rampant. 35.8 percent of Internet users have experienced viruses on more than five occasions in the past year. Only 3.6 percent of users report not having contracted viruses. Stealing of accounts and passwords is also rampant, and the worst offenses are experienced in Internet cafes: 56.5 percent of people whose accounts or passwords were stolen had them stolen in Internet cafes. 37.1 percent experienced this at home, either their own or the home of a friend. 24.7 percent experienced it at work, 17.5 percent at school, and 15.5 percent in public places such as libraries.

The Personal Life and Thoughts of Jack Ma

Family

December 15, 2005, marked the date of a major change in Alibaba's senior-level personnel. On that day, Jack Ma announced that an employee named Zhang Ying would be leaving the company. When he made this announcement, the auditorium was at first silent, then many in the audience began to cry.

Zhang Ying was Jack Ma's wife. She had been with the company from the beginning and rendered outstanding service. Her decision to leave the company was initially rejected by the board of directors; employees were also against it. Zhang Ying herself stood up to this pressure and slowly but surely persuaded the company to let her go. She told the company that this was not a decision made lightly and it was not Jack Ma's decision; it was made voluntarily on her own. "She feels in part that it is improper to have the CEO's wife there in the company," Ma tried to explain. "No matter what that person is doing, or how well, it looks funny." Outsiders assumed that the decision was taken because the company was maturing, transitioning from start-up to regular operations, and it was no longer appropriate to have the wife of the founder involved. Jack Ma himself saw it as a personal choice. "She has had no life of her own for years. She has no friends outside the company; she has spent all day every day, from the beginning, inside this business."

Ma and his wife, Zhang Ying, came to know each other in college. First acquaintances, then friends, then lovers, then man and wife, they have been together ever since. As the Chinese saying goes, they have been "immersed in the same juices," to the extent that they operate as one. Zhang Ying has always remained in the background, as a support to Jack Ma, but friends say that in the final analysis, the two rely on each other mutually and are total partners.

Their son is now in high school and shows great promise, at least with regard to his height. "He's already taller than I am!" exclaims Jack Ma, implying that perhaps the son long ago shucked off the concerns that kept Ma short. When Ma took his son to visit his own father, Ma jokingly told him, "See how well I'm raising my son? What happened when you were raising me?" Both men knew well that what had happened was the so-called Three Years of Natural Disaster and the ensuing Cultural Revolution. That it can be joked about today is a tribute to the resilience of the Chinese people.

Ma once took a question from reporters that stopped him in

his tracks, albeit briefly. The question was, "What are you planning for Valentine's Day [August 11]?" "I never celebrate Valentine's Day," he finally responded, then added that he really was too busy. One can understand the family life issues that this man's schedule might involve. Ma became a celebrity in 2005 when Alibaba acquired Yahoo! China. Chased by the media, his image became ubiquitous overnight. "I saw myself so often on the news that I got sick of myself," he later commented. He had always maintained a friendly relationship with members of the press, but now Jack Ma began to hold a grudge against them.

The person he could least neglect in his new celebrity status remained his wife. Like every successful man, Jack Ma has a woman behind him. He has indicated that there is not a moment he does not appreciate the "silent woman" by his side. Just how silent and supportive is this woman? To all appearances, she is the ultimate partner. In 1995, when Ma was first founding the company, he left his teaching position and threw himself into the crazy world of the Internet. Zhang Ying did not object. Instead, she helped him pull together the funds that formed the initial investment in the enterprise. In the single room that served as their first office, she would count each bit of money before spending it. Together Zhang Ying and Jack Ma created the first B2B Web page in the history of China's Internet.

By 2005, ten years had gone by and Alibaba's "family" had grown to more than two thousand employees; the business had in fact become a whale that even dared to swallow Yahoo! China. Zhang Ying decided it was time for her to take a break.

"In fact, she is not at all a silent-type woman," Jack Ma has emphasized when questioned about their relationship. "She is outstanding as a businesswoman as well as in her personal life. Professionally, she has done extremely well." Ma cannot conceal a sense of pride about her, but at the same time he is candid about who is boss. When asked, "If there is a conflict between the two of you, who sacrifices a little more?" His answer: "Naturally she does. Her help to me is total. No matter whether it is professionally or personally, she totally understands and supports me." In China, Jack Ma is considered to be a fortunate and very straightforward man.

Jack Ma's Idol, and His Martial Arts Avocation

Few in China can resist the addictive novels of Jin Yong (the pen name of Louis Cha); Jack Ma succumbed many years ago and has modeled his life on the martial code described in the stories. He has said he has "one idol in his heart," and that is Louis Cha. The author, who is now in his mid-eighties, has described his relationship with Jack Ma as one that transcends generational differences and is a genuine friendship.

Jack Ma emphatically describes his business strategy in *wu xia* terms, and much of his understanding of these terms comes directly from Cha's novels. As noted above, these combine martial arts with traditional Chinese culture and Chinese history. As we learned in the first chapter of this book, *wu xia* means something akin to "martial heroes," but with deeply resonating layers of cultural and philosophical meaning. Louis Cha lived most of his life in a British colony, and his exploration of these layers may reflect a profound longing for home, a home that for many decades he was unable to visit. Cha was born on February 6, 1924, in the same province that Jack Ma comes from: Zhejiang Province in southern China. His family name is Cha, though it is pronounced *za* in the Mandarin dialect. Knighted in 1981 by Queen Elizabeth, he is considered as much a British treasure as Chinese. The Cha family moved to Hong Kong, where Louis became one of the co-founders of the Hong Kong daily newspaper *Ming Pao* in

1959. He was the paper's first editor in chief, holding this position until 1993, when he retired. At the same time, Louis Cha began writing novels that soon made him the best-selling Chinese author in the world. Over one hundred million copies of his fifteen novels have officially been sold worldwide; this figure does not include pirated copies, which undoubtedly propel it to multiples of that number.

Five of these fifteen novels have been published in English. The most famous are *The Book and the Sword* (1955), *The Legend of the Condor Heroes* (1957), *Flying Fox of Snowy Mountain* (1959), and *The Deer and the Cauldron* (1969). Cha's last novel was written in 1972. Although Cha has received many and varied awards and honorary degrees, he began in 2007 a four-year course of study for his nonhonorary Ph.D. in Chinese history at the University of Cambridge.

Ma has read the novel *The Smiling Proud Wanderer* more times than any other book. The character he most appreciates is Feng Qingyang because he admires the way that character moves naturally, without premeditation. "He has thought through everything and internalized all moves in advance, so that he doesn't have to think about them. They are a part of him." As noted above, the word *move* is a special term in Chinese that signifies not just physical action but also mental discipline and focus. In martial arts training, the mental focus is as important, if not more so, than the physical result. This training is of cardinal importance to Jack Ma; his own moves in the realm of business are what have brought him recognition as a master of both strategy and well-timed action. Ma also compares himself to Feng the teacher—his mission in life is to bring along students who can surpass him. "I too come from the life of being a teacher. I most like it when my colleagues and my students can surpass me."

Among the *wu xia* concepts Jack Ma put into actual use in his business dealings is a sense of key values. Termed the "Six

Sacred Swords" in Alibaba parlance, these values are recognized by Western investment firms as bringing a major contribution to the bottom line. They are factored into an employee's performance ratings and so are reinforced in very real-world terms. The Six Swords derive originally from what are called the Nine Swords of Dugu, although nine were consolidated to six at Alibaba. (Dugu is a character in certain of Cha's novels, including *The Smiling Proud Wanderer*, *The Return of the Condor Heroes*, and *The Deer and the Cauldron*.)

Another saying that has been influential in Ma's thinking is "No moves trumps having moves." Once an opponent knows a person's moves, the opponent can use those against him. This relates to the fundamental idea in martial arts that a person's own strength can be turned against him, make him off balance, make him lose what had been his core defense. "Your opponent's strongest points are also his weakest," says Ma. "Most people think that the places to attack are those that show weakness. But the strengths are generally vulnerable. And the opposite is true: when everyone thinks there is a great danger in a particular strategy, you have to look closely for there may be great opportunities hiding inside."

In general, Ma is a contrarian who uses *wu xia* thinking to conceptualize scenarios that others might miss. In Western terms, the phrase "thinking outside the box" is a start on understanding the process, but it is relatively unidimensional compared to the multidimensional training that *wu xia* novels talk about. The training includes sustained focus on logical consequences. For example, one discipline is to visualize a far-focus and then a near-focus reality, then keep the vision in mind as you close your eyes and mentally move your reality from one place to another. The same is done in terms of time: training an internal eye to see different realities or scenarios at different times as factors change. Sports psychologists are aware of the benefits of mental training for physical performance; *wu xia* masters have used these tricks for centuries. Jack Ma has said that he sees the world as an enormous *weiqi* board, which similarly requires sustained logical thinking and focus. In using the moves and the mental training of *wu xia* masters, he has so far been able to apply ancient traditions to modern business with considerable success.

Natural-Born Performer

It is clear that Jack Ma has absorbed the lessons of martial arts to an unusual degree and applies them to his business strategy. It is equally clear to most who have heard Jack Ma speak that he is a natural-born performer.

Jack Ma has street smarts. He speaks to the heart of an issue in down-home language and will never be accused of a lack of self-confidence. As his friend Louis Cha says, "he strides the heavens like a white stallion." This is a take-off on the name Ma (meaning "horse"), but it also refers to the ancient Asian tradition of a white steed galloping through metaphysical realms at the head of his tribe. The white horse in Mongolian, Tibetan, and later Chinese philosophy is a being that can penetrate universes with a super-natural understanding. Not a businessman, MBA, programmer, nor engineer, Jack Ma is seen as someone who transcends these limited spheres. To his admirers, he strides the heavens.

It is refreshing, therefore, to hear Ma look at his own failures and derive lessons from them. He has made several about-face turns in business strategy. As a result, he keeps people guessing: he never seems to play by the conventional rules of the game. During the depths of the Internet "winter," Ma was secretly building Taobao. The cooperation with Yahoo! China has shocked many people in the field. In 2007 the entire company was reorganized prior to the listing of Alibaba.com on the Hong Kong stock exchange, and it will take some time for the industry to digest all the implications. Ma intends to have Alibaba join the ranks of the Fortune 500 in 2009. This latest gamble represents his biggest throw of the dice, and it is undeniable that many are waiting for him to fall from grace.

But Jack Ma has a track record as a winner. From an early age he liked a good fight, and he has kept that feisty attitude as an adult. At the same time, he has occasionally revealed a deeper sense of social responsibility, the desire to influence fundamental social change. One small anecdote illustrates this basic drive. It relates to the very first time Ma appeared on television, back in 1995. He recalls:

We had just moved our business in Hangzhou out of my home to a separate office. I would ride my bike back to the office at eight in the evening, after dinner. One night, I suddenly came across a bunch of people removing a manhole from over the water main in a street. There must have been five or six of these guys, standing around using a big wooden pole to pry it off. I assumed they were going to steal the cover and sell it as scrap metal for some money. The thing was, a few days earlier I had seen a story in the paper about how a child had fallen into one of these holes and drowned after someone took the manhole cover. So it upset me to see people stealing another cover. There were a number of them, however, and just one of me, plus they were big. I looked around and didn't see any policemen, and the few people nearby weren't taking any notice of this. So I rode on a little, then turned around and rode back, and I went back and forth like this, trying to decide what to do. Finally, I couldn't stand it any longer. I stopped near the men. I kept one foot on my pedal as I shouted at one of them, "You put that back!" I was thinking that if they charged me, I could run. I raised my fist at them as I shouted. So one of the men did walk over to me and he said, "What did you say?" That actually pleased me, because here they were responding. I said I wanted the men to put the manhole back in its place. The man then asked me what I thought they were doing. I said, "You're getting ready to take that manhole and you'd better put it back." As I said it, I thought it was a pretty stupid question on his part. Looking around, I finally realized that I was being filmed, on television. The TV station was doing a kind of psychology experiment, finding out what people would do about the theft, how long it would take for someone to stand up against it.

Wealth

On October 17, 2005, Jack Ma was listed as number four in a list of thirty names of the wealthiest entrepreneurs in the IT field in China. This ranking can be accomplished only by published reports of wealth, so it skips over privately held fortunes. Privately held wealth is able to operate in a freer manner than wealth that is subject to government scrutiny, and therefore some people feel it is a most unhappy thing to be put on the list. Ma finds it unfortunate for other reasons as well: the ranking creates a taste for money that affects people's attitudes. Worshiping wealth changes a community's sense of values.

This is not the fault merely of a list, of course. Ma and others feel that "we are living in an age of wealth" in which money is the yardstick for measuring life. As major fortunes are being made in China, a few senior businesspeople are beginning to be more philanthropic, some admittedly as a form of public penance, others because they understand the leverage their wealth can have on social change. Ma is ambivalent about philanthropy—but not about social change. He likes to think of himself not as a businessman but as an entrepreneur. To him, businessmen simply try to amass money, whereas entrepreneurs have the more important mission of bringing about positive change. "To businessmen and tradespeople, most everything is done in order to make money. Entrepreneurs, in contrast, create value. By creating value for society, they influence society. Making money is a fundamental attribute of entrepreneurs, but it is not your entire capability." Ma explained this attitude in a heartfelt response to an interviewer's questions on CCTV. He went on to say that he felt that philanthropists carry around a shadow over their activities: "When people chase after wealth, in a sense they also look down on it even while they are enjoying its pleasures. So those who engage in philanthropy are often a little conflicted. Remember that saying, 'So rich all he has left is money.' Few people talk about that saying right now, and the reason is that we are in a period in history when people are piling up capital and not wanting to think too much about its downside. The motivation to chase after money right now is very strong. As a result, people's attitude toward wealth is different from what it was before."

Another saying that Ma likes is "If we are going too fast, we need to slow down a little, wait for our souls to catch up." He feels that raw wealth is a not a good indicator of quality of life; an individual's well-being cannot be measured purely in terms of money. All of this sounds like protesting too much, since it is being said by a very wealthy man. But Ma quite specifically challenges the conventional attitude toward money. "A lot of people understand how to make money, and there are plenty of people in the world who can make money. There are not many who can influence the world, push society to make itself better. To make a great company, that's what you have to do." Wealth is incidental, as defined by the piling up of money, and Ma is ambitious enough to want to change China in a fundamental way: "Specifically, I want to change the history of China's e-commerce."

A Missionary for E-Commerce

In carrying out e-commerce, the most important thing is to keep doing what you are doing right now with passion, to keep it up.
—JACK MA

Alibaba is beginning to take its place among those companies that bring to mind an individual with a mission. With Matsushita, one thinks of its founder, Matsushita Konosuke; Whampoa brings to mind Li Ka-shing; Microsoft is Bill Gates. Jack Ma's mission is e-commerce.

When Ma speaks, his hands are always waving around. He never stands still but always moves as though preparing to attack. In any interview with the press, he takes the opportunity to proselytize for e-commerce. He wants to make sure that this newly arrived vehicle is daily more familiar to every person in China. He believes e-commerce will restructure the way all business and commerce are done, resulting in radical savings in energy, environment, and human effort. As a result, he has become known as a kind of spiritual proselytizer in China's world of business.

One narrowly defined example of e-commerce benefits to the Chinese business community is often summed up as "Chinese people vs. Wal-Mart." Wal-Mart buys in superlarge quantities and is thereby able to squeeze down prices of small suppliers. In China today, more than four-fifths of all business is conducted by small and medium-sized enterprises. Since there are an estimated 32 million such enterprises in the country, supplying cost-saving services to this needy group of customers is, in Jack Ma's opinion, not only good business but also good for the entire economy of China. At the same time, he feels it will be good for the world in streamlining business links, saving in areas where the extra funds can more profitably be put into innovation and a better world.

★ ★ ★

That, briefly, is the theory. In order to promote that theory, Ma has come up with a number of sound bites that press home the message:

★ We want to give commerce back to businesspeople; that is, allow businesspeople themselves to choose what they need, the language in which they need to operate, the technology they need to use.

★ E-commerce is a process that uses modern methods to increase trade opportunities, to raise the efficiency of production and trade, and to lower costs.

★ Even the most perfect product will not be accepted by the market unless it is useful to the market. If there are real benefits to businesspeople and enterprises, a product will fly. E-commerce has to deliver those real benefits.

★ The winners of e-commerce in the future will not be traditional enterprises, but they also will not be purely Internet companies. The future winners will merge the methods of both.

★ What makes us successful as a company is that we are only a step and a half ahead of others. The reason this is best is that products we put before the public can be adopted by them, actually used by them. People need to feel that our e-commerce tools are simple and easy. More than two steps ahead of people means you lose that immediate usefulness.

★ There are two aspects to e-commerce. One is voluntary, the other is forced. The establishment of trust systems belongs to the forced aspect. I tell everyone that when Alibaba members use the TrustPass, it's like the doctor forcing a sick person to take a certain medicine: "Here, take this, it will be good for you."

★ E-commerce has no "best" model. All it has is a model that is most suited to yourself. Alibaba is not so much an e-commerce company as we are an electronic services company.

★ You can't do e-commerce in one fell swoop—one shout and you all rise up. Building the systems is an incremental process.

★ SARS made everyone realize that e-commerce is good. E-commerce allowed business to go on without people infecting everyone else. That's not to say that SARS made e-commerce into something even better. It simply enabled recognition.

★ The two biggest problems in e-commerce right now are safety or the security of transactions, and trust. Of these, the more critical is trust.

★ The most attractive thing about e-commerce is its openness.

Keep It Up! Reorganization and IPO

n 2007 Alibaba underwent a major reorganization preparatory to raising money by listing part of the company on the Hong Kong stock exchange. An umbrella parent called the Alibaba Group became the repository for several of the affiliated Alibaba companies, including 75 percent of the B2B online marketplace called Alibaba.com. On November 6, 17 percent of Alibaba.com was sold to public shareholders, with 75 percent retained by the parent company, the Alibaba Group, and 8 percent by employees, management, and consultants.

The parent Alibaba Group is in turn owned 39 percent by Yahoo!, 29 percent by Softbank, and 32 percent by management and employees. Alibaba.com is incorporated in the Cayman Islands, a location of choice for many Asian companies. Hangzhou Alibaba Advertising Co., Ltd., is incorporated in the People's Republic of China and holds the Internet content provider (ICP) license that allows Alibaba to do its Internet business in China. With 80 percent of shares, Jack Ma is in control of Hangzhou Alibaba, and Simon Xie, one of the early founders of Alibaba, holds the other 20 percent. Without licenses from this China-based entity, Alibaba, as an offshore-based entity, could not operate as an Internet company within China.

To prepare for this reorganization, a new management team was installed at Alibaba in November 2006. The new CEO of Alibaba.com, in charge of all Alibaba's B2B business, is David Wei. Wei comes from outside the Alibaba fold: he previously headed China's largest home improvement retailer, so he understands the buying and selling side of the business from the customer perspective. A new CFO, Maggie Wu, was also hired from outside to handle Alibaba.com's finances. Wu previously was an audit partner at KPMG's Beijing office.

The Alibaba.com IPO represented the second largest Internet IPO in history, despite being a public offering for less than one-fifth of only one part of the Alibaba Group. The largest was that of Google, which raised $1.67 billion. After listing, Alibaba.com's stock soon traded at HKD 39.50, up from the offer price of HKD 13.50 ($1.74). As of mid-2008, Alibaba.com was trading in the neighborhood of HKD 10. Industry evaluations of the company overall are positive. Alibaba.com's paying customer base is increasing very quickly, it enjoys over 80 percent gross margins, its business model is working, and its cash flow is excellent.

These high marks can be attributed to the way in which Alibaba was reorganized prior to the listing. Lesser-margin businesses were kept outside the financials of the listed company. At the same time, the sister entities continue to contribute to the overall critical mass of Alibaba's business. Jack Ma is intent on allowing lower-margin businesses to look to a strategic future, rather than force them into the straitjacket of quarterly earnings reports. In general, the reorganization and the listing have been well received.

Three major investment banks shepherded the process of taking Alibaba into a new era: Goldman Sachs, Morgan Stanley, and Deutsche Bank. Jack Ma's martial arts moves may have provided the framework of the deal—the "bones," as it were—but the basic concept was helped considerably by the professional attention of these three. Alibaba.com was incorporated in September 2006 as a holding company for the B2B businesses of the Alibaba Group. Taobao, Alibaba, and Alipay were split off as separate entities, though still under the overarching structure of the Alibaba Group. Unlike the acquisition of Yahoo! China, which was accomplished privately and quickly and without the complexities of public scrutiny, the listing process was carefully guided by highly technical expertise.

Reorganizing the company to separate high-margin businesses from low-margin ones had the immediate effect of gaining a tremendous cushion of capital. The Alibaba Group has made no public decision regarding whether to inject other group assets into the Alibaba.com listed company. Separating the businesses may help the Alibaba Group pursue its strategic goal of dominating e-commerce-related activities, including marketplaces, payments, search, and advertising—in China and elsewhere—by allowing its unlisted units to focus on market growth rather than profitability. This is very much in line with Jack Ma's general philosophy.

Alibaba.com has entered a field that few but industry professionals understand very well. The activities of Internet companies include several key money-making components, including paid search, online marketplace, trade media, and social networking. Alibaba.com is involved in all of these. Its primary competitors in the search market in China are Baidu and Google. In the consumer online marketplace, the parent company is going head-to-head, most importantly, with eBay. Baidu and Alibaba.com both act as listing tools for small and medium-sized enterprises, but Baidu offers these companies exposure only in China, whereas Alibaba. com offers them global exposure. Baidu serves both wholesalers and retailers, whereas Alibaba.com serves only wholesalers. In the B2B online marketplace arena, Alibaba.com now holds 60 percent of its market share in China.

In industry jargon, Alibaba operates online networks that derive value from their members' interactions. Alibaba is said to be the clear market leader worldwide with a critical mass in what is known as a "network effects" business. The magical thing about network effects is that they grow themselves. Like a crystal or any other self-organizing structure, they self-accrete without having to be created laboriously, bit by bit. As a result, the idea of a network effects business fits perfectly with Jack Ma's renowned appreciation for the idea of being lazy.

The reality, however, is that there is nothing lazy about Alibaba. The network that Alibaba offers relates primarily to commerce, and selling that idea to customers requires tremendous sales force participation. In point of fact, Alibaba's is a labor-intensive model. The sales force at the company now totals more than twenty-five hundred people. Sales offices were opened in sixteen cities in China prior to 2007 and in another fourteen cities in 2007. As of June 30, 2007, the total number of full-time Alibaba employees came to forty-four hundred. Jack Ma and those employees run very hard to keep the coffers full.

The Business Model

Alibaba makes money by charging customers for membership services. Alibaba.com operates international (English-language) and domestic (Chinese-language) online marketplaces, which charge companies, primarily small companies, to list products online. Buyers can go online and browse these products for free: suppliers therefore have twenty-four-hour access to a global audience. As of June 2007, Alibaba.com hosted 2.4 million supplier storefronts, with, on average, 2.9 million new product listings per month. Buyers click on product listings and are taken to suppliers' storefronts. Buyers are allowed onsite for free, but Alibaba charges fees for services to sellers. Because of the free access, Alibaba states that "together our marketplaces form a community of more than 24 million registered users from over 200 countries and regions."

Some three-quarters of Alibaba.com's income derives from its international, English-language-based marketplace. One-quarter comes from the domestic, Chinese-language-based marketplace. The basic price of services in the English-language marketplace is, in 2008, around $6,500. Around twenty-two thousand China Suppliers are currently registered as members and pay this price. Alibaba started charging for its English-language marketplace services in the year 2000. The basic price of services in the China-language domestic marketplace is a little less than $400. Alibaba started charging for domestic services in 2002; now nearly 222,000 suppliers are currently registered and pay this price.

In addition to basic membership services, those companies that select additional value-added services are charged extra. For example, International TrustPass members pay $589 per year for TrustPass services. Some 13 percent of these are customers from the United States, 16 percent are from Hong Kong, 11 percent from Taiwan, 8 percent from India, and 6 percent from Korea. All contracts for value-added services for suppliers are for one to two years, and all must be paid in advance. This is highly beneficial to Alibaba's cash flow; revenues are amortized over the period for which they are contracted.

Alibaba's business model takes advantage of the fact that China has been and continues to be the primary product supplier to the world. As mentioned previously, some four-fifths of the companies supplying products to the world from China are small- and medium-sized enterprises, and there are about 32 million such enterprises in China. Of these, a small percentage, perhaps 2 to 3 million, actually export. Alibaba therefore focuses on the top of this enormous pyramid of small companies—in other words, those savvy and nimble enough to get their products to global markets. The rest of the 32 million companies, however, are also part of the process, for they supply to the top-of-the-pyramid global suppliers. These companies may also list on Alibaba, but for free. Alibaba provides a venue not just for paying suppliers but for any supplier who wants to post very basic information, gratis, on the site. It therefore is able to provide buyers with information on over 10 million suppliers.

Domestic trade within China among small and medium-sized enterprises, quite apart from exported goods, totaled some $530 billion in 2007. The market research firm iResearch estimates that this figure will continue to grow at 15 percent per year. The same organization estimates that the import and export trade volume of small enterprises in China was $1.7 trillion in 2007 and that it will continue to grow at 20 percent per year. These numbers are the base upon which Alibaba builds its business. Alibaba has already developed a critical mass of buyers and suppliers on its marketplace, which is the largest in the world.

Financials of the listed company are therefore excellent. Year-on-year growth in net income is forecast at over 200 percent in 2008, building on a similar increase in 2007, though declining to mere double digits in 2009 and 2010. Revenues increased 85 percent year-on-year in 2006 and 61 percent in the first half of 2007. Margins remain high, approaching 50 percent prior to stock-based compensation. Since members are fickle and the turnover rate remains high, the key to this ferocious growth is continued sales of memberships and value-added services to new members.

One might wonder why suppliers would pay to be listed on Alibaba if they could post their products for free. The reason relates to Alibaba's services. These include authentication and verification of buyers' credentials, cheaper access to the payment platform Alipay, help in creation of Web sites or storefronts, and ability to get to the front of the line in terms of response to customers' inquiries. One of the new services, which points to trends to come, is the ability to take out loans from the Industrial and Commercial Bank of China on the basis of one's trade volume on Alibaba. Overall, Alibaba's strategy is to convert nonpaying suppliers to paying ones by offering irresistible value-added benefits.

Large buyers such as Home Depot, Procter & Gamble, and Wal-Mart typically replace around 20 percent of the suppliers that sell to them every year. This degree of uncertainty is highly destabilizing to small suppliers. Alibaba has therefore served a useful function for all who need the stability of an ongoing market. At the same time, Alibaba is increasingly used by larger buyers as well, who do initial screening of offerings on the Internet. Typical buyers on Alibaba.com include importers, trading companies, the procurement departments of manufacturing companies, and the sourcing departments of retailers.

Alipay is a critical part of the Alibaba scheme. The company is not part of the listed Alibaba.com, but Alibaba.com receives fees if transactions are paid for via Alipay. As noted above, Alibaba.com receives 60 percent to 85 percent of the consequent fees. Monetizing transactions has been how eBay and other Internet companies make money. Alibaba has resisted a model that charges for every transaction, but by channeling payments through Alipay, Alibaba successfully earns a percentage of transactions as well. Whether or not Alibaba will start charging direct transaction fees remains to be seen. The relationship between Alibaba and Alipay makes it clear that as the digital convergence proceeds, the world will also witness a convergence of the financial and IT sectors. China's banking and financial industry is highly regulated. It is also in the midst of regulatory flux as Western banks enter the market and Chinese banks gear up for more challenging competition. As a Chinese company, Jack Ma's Alibaba is in a favorable position to benefit from the open environment of global finance as well as the protected environment of a Chinese home base.

Looking Forward

Creating Alibaba has required two key talents: an ability to recognize the direction of technology and a determination to force its pace. It required an ability to read future moves on the *weiqi* board: to understand how technology is linked to human social organization and how to leverage small moves into large consequences. As Alibaba moves farther into the global arena (possibly through a future affiliation with Microsoft), it will be interesting to see how Jack Ma plays his next moves. All eyes will be on the *wu xia* master. Whatever happens, the scrappy little boy turned master performer is not likely to disappoint his audience.

Jack Ma's Personal Chronology

(with Key Events in China's Recent History)

1911	End of imperial China's Qing dynasty
1937	Invasion of China by Japan and start of Anti-Japanese War
1945	End of World War II, including defeat of Japan in China
1945–49	Civil War in China between Communist Party and Kuomintang
1949	Founding of People's Republic of China on October 1 (start of Communist rule in China)

1958	Great Leap Forward (radical economic policies pursued by Mao Zedong)
1959–61	Three Years of Natural Disaster (famine in China)
Sept. 10, 1964	Jack Ma is born in Hangzhou, Zhejiang Province, China
1966–76	Cultural Revolution in China (intense social turmoil)
1972	Nixon goes to China
1976	Death of Chairman Mao Zedong; death of Premier Zhou Enlai
1979	Deng Xiaoping becomes the first Chinese leader to visit the United States
1984	Ma enters college at age twenty, after failing exam twice
1984–88	Ma spends four years at Hangzhou Normal College
1988–93	Ma spends five years teaching English at Hangzhou Electronics Technology College
Jan. 1994	Ma founds Haibo Translation Agency in Hangzhou
1995	Ma's first trip to the United States and contact with the Internet
Apr. 1995	Ma starts China Yellow Pages in Hangzhou
End 1995	Chinese government discourages media coverage of the Internet
Early 1996	*People's Daily* puts up a Web page on the Internet; media coverage is now allowed
1997	China Yellow Pages, founded by Ma, is sold to Hangzhou Telecom
1998–99	Ma spends fourteen months in Beijing, creating trade-related Web pages at Ministry of Foreign Trade

Jan. 15, 1999	Ma returns to Hangzhou with his team
Feb. 1999	Ma founds Alibaba at his home at Hangzhou's Lakeside Garden residential area
Oct. 1999	Goldman Sachs becomes lead investor in Alibaba, investing $5 million
Nov. 1999	First meeting between Masayoshi Son and Jack Ma, leading to $20 million in financing
2000	Nasdaq begins to plunge, leading to two-year dot-com bust; Alibaba is already well funded
Dec. 15, 2005	Zhang Ying, Jack Ma's wife, retires from Alibaba

Alibaba Chronology

February 1998

Zhang Chaoyang officially launches the portal Sohu.com in China; it is successfully listed on the Nasdaq exchange in 2000

December 1998

First online marketplace launched by Ma's team, operated as a bulletin board service (BBS) for businesses to post buy-and-sell trade leads

March 1999

Alibaba Web site is launched; team leader Jack Ma formally returns to Hangzhou from Beijing to found the business

June 1999

Jack Ma and eighteen other founders officially form the parent company Alibaba Group

July 1999

Alibaba China Control Shares Ltd. is established in Hong Kong

September 1999

Alibaba China, Alibaba's major operating subsidiary in China, is established to carry on the business of providing software and technology services for the operation of online B2B marketplaces, and Alibaba (China) Internet Technology Ltd. is set up in Hangzhou; Hong Kong serves as the headquarters of Alibaba Company and Hangzhou serves as headquarters for the China region

October 1999

Alibaba takes in $5 million in venture capital funding, with Goldman Sachs serving as lead underwriter

January 2000

Softbank in Japan, headed by Masayoshi Son, puts $20 million into the company, in Alibaba's second round of investment (prior to bursting of global dot-com bubble); Alibaba begins to expand internationally with headquarters in Hong Kong and offices in Silicon Valley, London, and elsewhere

October 2000

Gold Supplier membership is launched to serve China exporters

August 2001

International TrustPass membership launched to serve exporters outside China

December 2001

Alibaba becomes the world's first business Web site to exceed one million members

March 2002

China TrustPass membership launched to serve small and medium-sized enterprises engaging in domestic trade in China

July 2002

Keyword services launched on international marketplace

October 2002

Alibaba's Japanese Web site is launched with a full-scale campaign to take the Japanese market

End 2002

Company overall begins to realize a profit

May 2003

Taobao is created secretly through spring 2003 for consumer transactions in a C2C business

July 2003

Alibaba formally announces in Beijing that it is investing RMB 100 million in Taobao, as Jack Ma intends to break into the China domestic C2C market

August 2003

Taobao celebrates its 100th day on August 17; Ma announces that beginning on August 18, for the next three years Taobao will not charge for its transaction services, in order to compete with eBay-EachNet

October 2003

Alibaba establishes Alipay, a payment platform for transactions on the Internet

November 2003

TradeManager instant-messaging software is launched to enable users to communicate in real time

End 2003

Daily income reaches RMB 1 million; Taobao is deployed on a no-fee basis for domestic China online C2C business

May 2004

Taobao promotes its in-house Alipay, lowering risk of Internet transactions; at the same time begins a cooperation with China Industrial & Commercial Bank, Merchants Bank, and other banks

July 2004

Taobao announces it has become the China leader in the China C2C market; it declares it is going to continue the no-fee basis

End 2004

Alipay is launched as a separate company

January 2005

Taobao officially enters the Hong Kong market

March 2005

Keyword bidding launched on China marketplace; Alibaba Company and the China Industrial and Commercial Bank reach a strategic cooperation agreement

April 2005

Taobao and Sohu announce they have become strategic partners

June 2005

Jack Ma of Alibaba and Ma Weihua of Merchants Bank sign a cooperative agreement in Shenzhen

August 2005

Alibaba joins with Yahoo! China, receiving an investment of $1 billion from Yahoo! China and ceding 40 percent of shares and 35 percent of voting rights

November 2005

Yahoo! Alibaba announces a new search engine; Ma announces that Alibaba is moving confidently into search engine territory

March 2006

Alibaba and China Agricultural Bank hold a joint press conference announcing they are joining hands in payment systems for B2B business

May 2006

Alibaba announces that it is formally entering the B2C realm, with Taobao as its platform

September 20, 2006

Alibaba begins a major reorganization in preparation for launching an IPO on the Hong Kong stock market; Alibaba.com Ltd. is incorporated in the Cayman Islands; Alibaba.com Investment Holding Ltd. is incorporated in the British Virgin Islands

October 5, 2006

Alibaba.com China Ltd. is incorporated in Hong Kong

December 7, 2006

Hangzhou Alibaba Advertising Co., Ltd., aka Alibaba Hangzhou, is established in China with two shareholders, Jack Ma and Simon Xie

January 2, 2007

Alibaba.com Investment Holding Ltd. acquires the entire equity interest in Alibaba.com, Inc. from Alibaba Group for cash consideration of approximately $3.2 million, which represents the net asset value of the entity as of December 31, 2006; Alibaba.com China Ltd. acquires the entire equity interest in the holding company Inter Network Technology Ltd. from Alibaba.com China Holding Ltd., a subsidiary of Alibaba Group, for consideration of $1 (RMB 8) (Inter Network Technology Ltd.'s major asset is the entire equity interest in Alibaba [Shanghai] Technology Co., Ltd., an inactive company which substantially ceases operations on a permanent basis); Alibaba.com Investment Holding Ltd. acquires the entire equity interest in Alibaba Hong Kong from Alibaba Group for consideration of $1 (RMB 8)

January 17, 2007

Alibaba.com China Ltd. acquires the entire equity interests in Alibaba Software from Alibaba.com China Holding Ltd., a subsidiary of Alibaba Group, for cash consideration of $6 million (RMB 46.7 million), which represents the registered capital of the entity at the time of the transfer

April 11, 2007

Alibaba.com China Ltd. acquires the entire equity interests in Alibaba China from Alibaba.com China Holding Ltd., a subsidiary of Alibaba Group, for cash consideration of $14 million (RMB 108.2 million), which represents the registered capital of the entity at the time of the transfer

May 14, 2007

Alibaba.com Investment Holding Ltd. acquires all equity interest in Alibaba.com Taiwan Holding Ltd. from Alibaba Group for consideration of $1 (RMB 8)

May 23, 2007

Alibaba.com Investment Holding Ltd. acquires all equity interest in Alibaba.com Japan Investment Holding Ltd. from Alibaba Group for consideration of $1 (RMB 8)

June 4, 2007

Alibaba.com Japan Investment Holding Ltd. acquires all equity interest in Alibaba.com Japan Holding Ltd. from Alibaba Group for consideration of $1 (RMB 8)

June 30, 2007

Alibaba Hangzhou acquires all assets, liabilities and operations related to the B2B business owned by Zhejiang Alibaba E-Commerce Co., Ltd., an entity controlled by Alibaba Group, for consideration of RMB 0.1 million (Zhejiang Alibaba E-Commerce Co., Ltd. currently operates as an ICP company for Alipay)

July 10, 2007

Alibaba.com China Ltd. acquires all equity interest in Beijing Sinya Online Information Technology Co. Ltd. from Alibaba.com China Holding Ltd., a subsidiary of Alibaba Group, for consideration of $1 (RMB 8)

November 6–7, 2007

IPO raises HKD 13.1 billion; shares close at HKD 39.50, valuing company at roughly $26 billion; the IPO represents the largest Internet IPO in Asia and second largest globally, after Google

Glossary of Names

CHA, Louis, aka Jin Yong (*see* Jin Yong)

CHEN Tianqiao   CEO of Shanda Inc., an interactive online gaming company based in Shanghai; one of China's media billionaires

DENG Xiaoping   De facto leader of the People's Republic of China from 1978 to the early 1990s. Helped guide China in its opening to the outside world; died in 1997 at age ninety-two

DING Lei (William)   Founder of NetEase.com (originally a portal, now a gaming titan); was briefly known as richest man in China when company listed on Nasdaq; estimated worth now around $1.1 billion

FILO, David   Co-founder of Yahoo! together with Jerry Yang when the two were graduate students at Stanford

JIANG Nanchun   CEO of Focus Media, company in online Interactive Entertainment; in 2005 regarded as one of the ten richest men in China, since his interactive online gaming company was listed on the Nasdaq exchange

JIN Yong Pen name of Louis Cha, author of martial arts novels in the *wu xia* genre; scion of a major family in southern China who was born in China in 1924 and emigrated to Hong Kong, where he founded and ran the *Ming Pao* daily; family roots are the same region of China as the homeland of Jack Ma

LI Yanhong CEO of the company Baidu, the main Chinese-language search engine firm in China, listed on the Nasdaq exchange

LIANG Jianzhang CEO of Youcheng

LONG Yong Tu Board member of Alibaba.com; a major public figure in China, key in leading the negotiations for China's accession to the WTO; currently dean of the School of International Relations and Public Affairs at Fudan University and secretary-general of Boao Forum for Asia, a nonprofit organization committed to promoting economic integration among Asian countries

MA Huateng CEO of Tengxun

MA Yun (Jack) Founder of Alibaba in 1999, now chairman and nonexecutive director of Alibaba.com after the reorganization of 2007; lead founder of Alibaba Group and chairman and CEO of Alibaba Group since its inception in 1999, responsible for the overall strategy and focus of Alibaba Group; member of the APEC Business Advisory Council, established by the Asia-Pacific Economic Cooperation in 1995 as a vehicle for formalizing private sector participation in APEC; expected to spend 20 to 30 percent of his time on strategic management of Alibaba after the reorganization and IPO

MAO Zedong, aka Mao Tse-tung Born 1893, died 1976; chairman of the Chinese Communist Party 1945–76

NIU Gensheng Board member of Alibaba.com; chairman of the Remuneration Committee; grew up in Inner Mongolia, where he founded the Niu-Meng Dairy, China's largest milk-products company; major business figure in China

OKADA, Satoshi Nonexecutive director of Alibaba.com, Softbank representative; EVP of the Softbank Group's e-Commerce Business Planning in Japan since April 2000; prior to that, held various management positions within the Softbank Group

SHAO Yipo CEO of EachNet, eBay's partner in China prior to entry of Tom.com

SON, Masayoshi Founder of Softbank, a leading digital information company headquartered in Japan, investor in IT companies; Korean by heritage and before that Chinese by ethnic place of origin; raised as a social outcast in Japan, he went to the United States and began to make a fortune in the mid-1970s, then returned to Japan, where he founded Softbank; major investor in both Yahoo! and Alibaba

TSAI Chung (Joseph) Nonexecutive director of Alibaba.com; one of the founders, as well as a director and CFO, of Alibaba Group; holds a bachelor's degree in economics and East Asian studies from Yale University and a law degree from Yale Law School; following the global offering (2007), remains an executive director of the Alibaba Group and is expected to spend 30 percent to 50 percent of his time involved in the strategic management of the company

TSOU Kai-Lien (Rose) Nonexecutive director of Alibaba.com; currently senior vice president of Yahoo! Asia

TSUEI Tien Yuan (Andrew) Nonexecutive director of Alibaba. com, also appointed a nonexecutive director of Taobao Holding Ltd. in May 2007; formerly senior vice president of Wal-Mart Stores, Inc.

WANG Leilei Group president of Tom.com Internet

WANG Yan CEO and president of Sina, a China portal (sina.com)

WANG Zhidong Former CEO of Sina, a Chinese portal; attended Peking University, where he formally studied radio electronics but studied computers on his own; famous for shutting himself away in a tiny apartment in 1991 to write the first Chinese-language software for PCs; began writing software for the Internet; at end of 1998, merged his firm with a Silicon Valley–based Chinese portal set up by three Taiwanese students from Stanford and renamed the site Sina, which was listed on the Nasdaq exchange

WEI Zhe (David)   CEO of Alibaba.com after the reorganization of 2007; joined Alibaba Group in November 2006 as president of the B2B business division and executive vice president of Alibaba Group; president (from 2002 to 2006) and CFO (from 2000 to 2002) of B&Q China, a subsidiary of Kingfisher PLC, a leading home improvement retailer in Europe and Asia; holds a bachelor degree in international business management from Shanghai International Studies University

WU Wei (Maggie)   An executive director and chief financial officer of Alibaba.com since July 2007; previously an audit partner for fifteen years at KPMG's Beijing office; holds a bachelor's degree in accounting from Capital University of Economics and Business

XIE Shi Huang (Simon)   Co-owner of Hangzhou Alibaba with Jack Ma; holds 20 percent of shares in this company, which is officially licensed to do Alibaba's Internet business in China; one of the early founders of Alibaba and worked with Jack Ma (prior to founding Alibaba) at MOFTEC in Beijing, serving as financial controller; holds a bachelor's degree in engineering from Shenyang University of Technology

YANG, Jerry   Chinese-American founder of Yahoo! (Chinese name is Yang Zhiyuan); currently CEO of the company again, succeeding Terry Semel

ZHANG Chaoyang (Charles)   Founder and CEO of Sohu in China; born in 1964 in Xi'an, Shaanxi Province; received a B.A. from Qinghua University in Beijing; won a scholarship in 1986 and joined a privileged group of Chinese students at MIT, where he received a Ph.D. in experimental physics; returned to China in 1995 and started a company that was later renamed Sohu and that launched the sohu.com Web site in February 1998, which was taken public on Nasdaq in 2000; has gone on to achieve recognition as a

Global Leader of Tomorrow by the World Economic Forum and a fellow architect of the future by such people as Jack Ma

ZHOU Hongwei   CEO of 3721, company founded in late 1998 and since 1999 a market leader for Chinese keyword search service in China

Glossary of Terms

Alibaba China Alibaba (China) Technology Co., Ltd., a wholly owned subsidiary of Alibaba.com

Alibaba Group Controlling shareholder in Alibaba.com, incorporated in Cayman Islands, holds numerous Alibaba family subsidiaries and affiliates; is 39 percent owned by Yahoo!, 29 percent owned by Softbank, and 32 percent owned by management and employees of Alibaba; the Alibaba Group in turn owns 75 percent of Alibaba.com, recently listed on the Hong Kong stock exchange

Alibaba Hangzhou Hangzhou Alibaba Advertising Co., Ltd., which holds the Internet licenses necessary for doing Internet business inside the PRC

Alibaba Hangzhou shareholders   Jack Ma (80 percent) and Simon Xie (20 percent)

Alibaba Hong Kong   Alibaba.com Hong Kong Ltd., a wholly owned subsidiary of Alibaba.com

Alibaba.com   The world's largest online marketplace for global and domestic China trade, a corporation that is listed on the Hong Kong stock market as of November 2007

Alibaba.com Corporation management shareholders   Jack Ma (chairman, director, and CEO of Alibaba.com Corporation); Joseph Tsai (director and CFO of Alibaba.com Corporation); John Wu (chief technology officer of Alibaba.com Corporation); and Li Qi (COO of Alibaba.com Corporation)

Alipay   The online payment business operated by Zhejiang Alipay Network Technology Co., Ltd. and Alipay Software (Shanghai) Co., Ltd., each a wholly owned subsidiary of Alibaba Group, and Zhejiang Alibaba E-Commerce Co., Ltd., a consolidated affiliate of Alibaba Group

Alisoft   The Internet-based business software business operated by Alibaba Software (Shanghai) Co., Ltd., a wholly owned subsidiary of Alibaba Group; partners include Microsoft, Oracle, Cisco, Sun, and Dell

B2B   Business to business, a business model whereby businesses sell to businesses, as distinguished from B2C (business to consumer) and C2C (consumer to consumer)

C2C   Consumer to consumer, a business model that allows consumers to buy and sell from each other directly

CNNIC   China Internet Network Information Center (CNNIC), the state network information center of China, founded as a nonprofit organization on June 3, 1997; reports to the Ministry of Information Industry (MII) with respect to daily business; administratively operated by Chinese Academy of Sciences

CSRC   China Securities Regulatory Commission

Dangdang   Company in the business of online book selling

HKD Hong Kong dollars, the lawful currency of Hong Kong; exchange rate in early 2008: $1 = HKD 7

Hong Kong public offering of Alibaba The offer of initially 128,835,500 shares for subscription by the public in Hong Kong, November 2007

ICBC Industrial and Commercial Bank of China Ltd.

IPO Initial public offering; in the case of Alibaba.com, the offering to the public made on November 6, 2007, on the Hong Kong stock exchange of 17 percent of the company after reorganization (offering did not include Taobao, Alipay, or other parts of the parent company known as the Alibaba Group)

Joint bookrunners of Alibaba.com IPO Goldman Sachs (Asia) LLC, Morgan Stanley Asia Ltd., and Deutsche Bank AG, Hong Kong branch

Journey to the West Chinese novel from the late sixteenth century, attributed to the author Wu Cheng'en; describes the travels to India of a priest and his companions, including Monkey and Pig

Joyo Company that engages in online B2C business, such as supply of videos and other products

MII Ministry of Information Industries: a megaministry created out of several other ministries in 1998, including Ministry of Post and Telecommunication and Ministry of Electronic Industries; regulates telecom companies

Ministry of Public Security The PRC Ministry of Public Security

MOFCOM or MOFTEC The PRC Ministry of Commerce or its predecessor, the Ministry of Foreign Trade and Economic Cooperation

MOFERT Ministry of Foreign Economic Relations and Trade, predecessor of MOFCOM or MOFTEC

National People's Congress The National People's Congress of the PRC, the country's highest state body and only legislative house; has had a largely symbolic role, though its standing committee has a quasi-judicial function

New M&A rule The Provisions Regarding Mergers and Acquisitions of Domestic Enterprises by Foreign Investors, promulgated on August 8, 2006, by MOFCOM, CSRC, and four other PRC regulatory agencies

Outlaws of the Marsh   Chinese novel, also known as *Water Margin* and *All Men Are Brothers*; sixteenth-century consolidation of Chinese folklore dating from the twelfth century about 108 heroes whose stronghold is Liang Shan (Mount Liang); loosely based on the historical bandit Song Jiang and his fellow outlaws

Paying members   Suppliers of products who subscribe to fee-based membership packages of Alibaba's international and China marketplaces

PBOC   The People's Bank of China, central bank of the PRC

PRC   People's Republic of China

PRC government   The central or state government of the PRC, including all governmental subdivisions

Renminbi (RMB)   Lawful currency of the PRC; exchange rate in early 2008: $1 = RMB 7.3

Reorganization   The restructuring undertaken by the Alibaba Group in late 2007, prior to the listing of Alibaba.com on the Hong Kong stock exchange

SAFE   The PRC State Administration of Foreign Exchange

SAIC   The PRC State Administration for Industry and Commerce

SARS   Severe acute respiratory syndrome, a highly contagious form of atypical pneumonia

SMEs   Small and medium enterprises, in China said to number between 31 million and 32 million

SoftBank   SoftBank Corp., founded and headed by Masayoshi Son

State Council   The State Council of the PRC, chief administrative authority of the country, composed of around fifty members but guided by the Standing Committee

Taijiquan (tai chi chuan, tai ji quan)   Form of martial arts practice that incorporates a philosophy of extremes as balanced into oneness; *quan* means "fists" or "hands" and *taiji* refers to "ultimate extremes"; discipline uses not just hands and body but more importantly mental focus

Taobao The consumer e-commerce business operated by Tao Bao (China) Software Co., Ltd., a wholly owned subsidiary of Alibaba Group

Telecom License Measures The Administrative Measures for Telecommunications Businesses Operating Licenses, promulgated by the MII on December 26, 2001, and effective as of January 1, 2002

Telecommunications Regulations The Telecommunications Regulations of the PRC, issued by the State Council on September 25, 2000

TradeManager Alibaba's instant-messaging tool for online communication

TrustPass A paid service on the Alibaba.com Web site, begun in March 2002; offers various ways to validate and rank credit-ratings and trustworthiness of companies

WTO World Trade Organization; China gained full membership in 2007

Wu xia Martial arts masters, also the genre of martial arts novels and films; term implies a realm of chivalrous conduct and vigorous physical training that is for a lofty purpose

Yahoo! Yahoo! Inc., the Internet search engine and portal company founded by Jerry Yang and David Filo, incorporated in the United States

Yahoo! China The Internet search engine and portal business operated by Inter China Software (Beijing) Co., Ltd., Beijing Yahoo! Information Technology Co., Ltd., Beijing Yahoo! Consulting Services Co., Ltd., and Alibaba Technology (Beijing) Co., Ltd., each a wholly owned subsidiary of Alibaba Group; and Beijing Alibaba Information Technology Co., Ltd., a consolidated affiliate of Alibaba Group

Index